# MARTIN LUTHER

# MARTIN LUTHER

Sally Stepanek

### CHELSEA HOUSE PUBLISHERS
### PHILADELPHIA

SENIOR EDITOR: William P. Hansen
ASSOCIATE EDITORS: John Haney
                   Richard Mandell
                   Marian W. Taylor
EDITORIAL COORDINATOR: Karyn Gullen Browne
EDITORIAL STAFF: Pierre Hauser
                 Perry Scott King
                 Howard Ratner
                 Alma Rodriguez-Sokol
                 John Selfridge
                 Bert Yaeger
ART DIRECTOR: Susan Lusk
LAYOUT: Irene Friedman
ART ASSISTANTS: Noreen Lamb
                Carol McDougall
                Victoria Tomaselli
COVER ILLUSTRATION: Neil Waldman
PICTURE RESEARCH: Diane Wallace

    7  9  8  6

Library of Congress Cataloging in Publication Data

Stepanek, Sally. MARTIN LUTHER

    (World Leaders past & present)
    Bibliography: p.
    Includes index.
    1. Luther, Martin, 1483–1546—Juvenile literature.
2. Reformation—Biography—Juvenile literature.
[1. Luther, Martin, 1483–1546.  2. Reformers]
I. Title.  II. Series.
BR325.S718    1986        284.1'092'4 [B] [92]  85—27985

ISBN 0-87754-538-3
      0-7910-0652-2 (pbk.)

Photos courtesy of Art Resource, The Bettmann Archive, The
Metropolitan Museum of Art, The New York Public Library.

# Contents

John Adams
John Quincy Adams
Konrad Adenauer
Alexander the Great
Salvador Allende
Marc Antony
Corazon Aquino
Yasir Arafat
King Arthur
Hafez al-Assad
Kemal Atatürk
Attila
Clement Attlee
Augustus Caesar
Menachem Begin
David Ben-Gurion
Otto von Bismarck
Léon Blum
Simon Bolívar
Cesare Borgia
Willy Brandt
Leonid Brezhnev
Julius Caesar
John Calvin
Jimmy Carter
Fidel Castro
Catherine the Great
Charlemagne
Chiang Kai-Shek
Winston Churchill
Georges Clemenceau
Cleopatra
Constantine the Great
Hernán Cortés
Oliver Cromwell
Georges-Jacques
  Danton
Jefferson Davis
Moshe Dayan
Charles de Gaulle
Eamon De Valera
Eugene Debs
Deng Xiaoping
Benjamin Disraeli
Alexander Dubček
François & Jean-Claude
  Duvalier
Dwight Eisenhower
Eleanor of Aquitaine
Elizabeth I
Faisal
Ferdinand & Isabella
Francisco Franco
Benjamin Franklin

Frederick the Great
Indira Gandhi
Mohandas Gandhi
Giuseppe Garibaldi
Amin & Bashir Gemayel
Genghis Khan
William Gladstone
Mikhail Gorbachev
Ulysses S. Grant
Ernesto "Che" Guevara
Tenzin Gyatso
Alexander Hamilton
Dag Hammarskjöld
Henry VIII
Henry of Navarre
Paul von Hindenburg
Hirohito
Adolf Hitler
Ho Chi Minh
King Hussein
Ivan the Terrible
Andrew Jackson
James I
Wojciech Jaruzelski
Thomas Jefferson
Joan of Arc
Pope John XXIII
Pope John Paul II
Lyndon Johnson
Benito Juárez
John Kennedy
Robert Kennedy
Jomo Kenyatta
Ayatollah Khomeini
Nikita Khrushchev
Kim Il Sung
Martin Luther King, Jr.
Henry Kissinger
Kublai Khan
Lafayette
Robert E. Lee
Vladimir Lenin
Abraham Lincoln
David Lloyd George
Louis XIV
Martin Luther
Judas Maccabeus
James Madison
Nelson & Winnie
  Mandela
Mao Zedong
Ferdinand Marcos
George Marshall

Mary, Queen of Scots
Tomáš Masaryk
Golda Meir
Klemens von Metternich
James Monroe
Hosni Mubarak
Robert Mugabe
Benito Mussolini
Napoléon Bonaparte
Gamal Abdel Nasser
Jawaharlal Nehru
Nero
Nicholas II
Richard Nixon
Kwame Nkrumah
Daniel Ortega
Mohammed Reza Pahlavi
Thomas Paine
Charles Stewart
  Parnell
Pericles
Juan Perón
Peter the Great
Pol Pot
Muammar el-Qaddafi
Ronald Reagan
Cardinal Richelieu
Maximilien Robespierre
Eleanor Roosevelt
Franklin Roosevelt
Theodore Roosevelt
Anwar Sadat
Haile Selassie
Prince Sihanouk
Jan Smuts
Joseph Stalin
Sukarno
Sun Yat-sen
Tamerlane
Mother Teresa
Margaret Thatcher
Josip Broz Tito
Toussaint L'Ouverture
Leon Trotsky
Pierre Trudeau
Harry Truman
Queen Victoria
Lech Walesa
George Washington
Chaim Weizmann
Woodrow Wilson
Xerxes
Emiliano Zapata
Zhou Enlai

CHELSEA HOUSE PUBLISHERS

# ON LEADERSHIP
### Arthur M. Schlesinger, jr.

LEADERSHIP, it may be said, is really what makes the world go round. Love no doubt smooths the passage; but love is a private transaction between consenting adults. Leadership is a public trans-action with history. The idea of leadership affirms the capacity of individuals to move, inspire and mobilize masses of people so that they act together in pursuit of an end. Sometimes leadership serves good purposes, sometimes bad; but whether the end is benign or evil, great leaders are those men and women who leave their personal stamp on history.

Now, the very concept of leadership implies the proposition that individuals can make a difference. This proposition has never been universally accepted. From classical times to the present day, eminent thinkers have regarded individuals as no more than the agents and pawns of larger forces, whether the gods and goddesses of the ancient world or, in the modern era, race, class, nation, the dialectic, the will of the people, the spirit of the times, history itself. Against such forces, the individual dwindles into insignificance.

So contends the thesis of historical determinism. Tolstoy's great novel *War and Peace* offers a famous statement of the case. Why, Tolstoy asked, did millions of men in the Napoleonic wars, denying their human feelings and their common sense, move back and forth across Europe slaughtering their fellows? "The war," Tolstoy answered, "was bound to happen simply because it was bound to happen." All prior history predetermined it. As for leaders, they, Tolstoy said, "are but the labels that serve to give a name to an end and, like labels, they have the least possible connection with the event." The greater the leader, "the more conspicuous the inevitability and the predestination of every act he commits." The leader, said Tolstoy, is "the slave of history."

Determinism takes many forms. Marxism is the determinism of class, Nazism the determinism of race. But the idea of men and women as the slaves of history runs athwart the deepest human instincts. Rigid determinism abolishes the idea of human freedom—the assumption of free choice that underlies every move we make, every word we speak, every thought we think. It abolishes the idea of human responsibility, since it is manifestly unfair to reward or punish people for actions that are by definition beyond their control. No one can live consistently by any deterministic creed. The Marxist states prove this themselves by their extreme susceptibility to the cult of leadership.

More than that, history refutes the idea that individuals make no difference. In December 1931 a British politician crossing Park Avenue in New York City between 76th and 77th Streets around ten-thirty at night looked in the wrong direction and was knocked down by an automobile—a moment, he later recalled, of a man aghast, a world aglare: "I do not understand why I was not broken like an eggshell or squashed like a gooseberry." Fourteen months later an American politician, sitting in an open car in Miami, Florida, was fired on by an assassin; the man beside him was hit. Those who believe that individuals make no difference to history might well ponder whether the next two decades would have been the same had Mario Contasini's car killed Winston Churchill in 1931 and Giuseppe Zangara's bullet killed Franklin Roosevelt in 1933. Suppose, in addition, that Adolf Hitler had been killed in the street fighting during the Munich *Putsch* of 1923 and that Lenin had died of typhus during the First World War. What would the 20th century be like now?

For better or for worse, individuals do make a difference. "The notion that a people can run itself and its affairs anonymously," wrote the philosopher William James, "is now well known to be the silliest of absurdities. Mankind does nothing save through initiatives on the part of inventors, great or small, and imitation by the rest of us—these are the sole factors in human progress. Individuals of genius show the way, and set the patterns, which common people then adopt and follow."

Leadership, James suggests, means leadership in thought as well as in action. In the long run, leaders in thought may well make the greater difference to the world. But, as Woodrow Wilson once said, "Those only are leaders of men, in the general eye, who lead in action. . . . It is at their hands that new thought gets its translation into the crude language of deeds." Leaders in thought often invent in solitude and obscurity, leaving to later generations the tasks of imitation. Leaders in action—the leaders portrayed in this series—have to be effective in their own time.

And they cannot be effective by themselves. They must act in response to the rhythms of their age. Their genius must be adapted, in a phrase of William James's, "to the receptivities of the moment." Leaders are useless without followers. "There goes the mob," said the French politician hearing a clamor in the streets. "I am their leader. I must follow them." Great leaders turn the inchoate emotions of the mob to purposes of their own. They seize on the opportunities of their time, the hopes, fears, frustrations, crises, potentialities.

8

They succeed when events have prepared the way for them, when the community is waiting to be aroused, when they can provide the clarifying and organizing ideas. Leadership ignites the circuit between the individual and the mass and thereby alters history.

It may alter history for better or for worse. Leaders have been responsible for the most extravagant follies and most monstrous crimes that have beset suffering humanity. They have also been vital in such gains as humanity has made in individual freedom, religious and racial tolerance, social justice and respect for human rights.

There is no sure way to tell in advance who is going to lead for good and who for evil. But a glance at the gallery of men and women in *World Leaders—Past and Present* suggests some useful tests.

One test is this: do leaders lead by force or by persuasion? By command or by consent? Through most of history leadership was exercised by the divine right of authority. The duty of followers was to defer and to obey. "Theirs not to reason why,/ Theirs but to do and die." On occasion, as with the so-called "enlightened despots" of the 18th century in Europe, absolutist leadership was animated by humane purposes. More often, absolutism nourished the passion for domination, land, gold and conquest and resulted in tyranny.

The great revolution of modern times has been the revolution of equality. The idea that all people should be equal in their legal condition has undermined the old structures of authority, hierarchy and deference. The revolution of equality has had two contrary effects on the nature of leadership. For equality, as Alexis de Tocqueville pointed out in his great study *Democracy in America*, might mean equality in servitude as well as equality in freedom.

"I know of only two methods of establishing equality in the political world," Tocqueville wrote. "Rights must be given to every citizen, or none at all to anyone . . . save one, who is the master of all." There was no middle ground "between the sovereignty of all and the absolute power of one man." In his astonishing prediction of 20th-century totalitarian dictatorship, Tocqueville explained how the revolution of equality could lead to the "*Führerprinzip*" and more terrible absolutism than the world had ever known.

But when rights are given to every citizen and the sovereignty of all is established, the problem of leadership takes a new form, becomes more exacting than ever before. It is easy to issue commands and enforce them by the rope and the stake, the concentration camp and the *gulag*. It is much harder to use argument and achievement to overcome opposition and win consent. The Founding Fathers of the United States understood the difficulty. They believed that history had given them the opportunity to decide, as

Alexander Hamilton wrote in the first Federalist Paper, whether men are indeed capable of basing government on "reflection and choice, or whether they are forever destined to depend . . . on accident and force."

Government by reflection and choice called for a new style of leadership and a new quality of followership. It required leaders to be responsive to popular concerns, and it required followers to be active and informed participants in the process. Democracy does not eliminate emotion from politics; sometimes it fosters demagoguery; but it is confident that, as the greatest of democratic leaders put it, you cannot fool all of the people all of the time. It measures leadership by results and retires those who overreach or falter or fail.

It is true that in the long run despots are measured by results too. But they can postpone the day of judgment, sometimes indefinitely, and in the meantime they can do infinite harm. It is also true that democracy is no guarantee of virtue and intelligence in government, for the voice of the people is not necessarily the voice of God. But democracy, by assuring the rights of opposition, offers built-in resistance to the evils inherent in absolutism. As the theologian Reinhold Niebuhr summed it up, "Man's capacity for justice makes democracy possible, but man's inclination to injustice makes democracy necessary."

A second test for leadership is the end for which power is sought. When leaders have as their goal the supremacy of a master race or the promotion of totalitarian revolution or the acquisition and exploitation of colonies or the protection of greed and privilege or the preservation of personal power, it is likely that their leadership will do little to advance the cause of humanity. When their goal is the abolition of slavery, the liberation of women, the enlargement of opportunity for the poor and powerless, the extension of equal rights to racial minorities, the defense of the freedoms of expression and opposition, it is likely that their leadership will increase the sum of human liberty and welfare.

Leaders have done great harm to the world. They have also conferred great benefits. You will find both sorts in this series. Even "good" leaders must be regarded with a certain wariness. Leaders are not demigods; they put on their trousers one leg after another just like ordinary mortals. No leader is infallible, and every leader needs to be reminded of this at regular intervals. Irreverence irritates leaders but is their salvation. Unquestioning submission corrupts leaders and demeans followers. Making a cult of a leader is always a mistake. Fortunately hero worship generates its own antidote. "Every hero," said Emerson, "becomes a bore at last."

The signal benefit the great leaders confer is to embolden the rest of us to live according to our own best selves, to be active, insistent, and resolute in affirming our own sense of things. For great leaders attest to the reality of human freedom against the supposed inevitabilities of history. And they attest to the wisdom and power that may lie within the most unlikely of us, which is why Abraham Lincoln remains the supreme example of great leadership. A great leader, said Emerson, exhibits new possibilities to all humanity. "We feed on genius. . . . Great men exist that there may be greater men."

Great leaders, in short, justify themselves by emancipating and empowering their followers. So humanity struggles to master its destiny, remembering with Alexis de Tocqueville: "It is true that around every man a fatal circle is traced beyond which he cannot pass; but within the wide verge of that circle he is powerful and free; as it is with man, so with communities."

—*New York*

# 1

# The Dissident

*Here I stand; I can do no other.
God help me. Amen.*
—MARTIN LUTHER
speaking at the Diet of Worms,
April 18, 1521

On April 17, 1521, a young theologian named Martin Luther was led into the great hall of a bishop's palace in Worms, Germany. Before him sat the Holy Roman Emperor Charles V, with his princes, cardinals, archbishops, and knights. Walking beside Luther, who was an Augustinian friar and professor of Bible studies at the University of Wittenberg, were two German soldiers who had escorted him through the crowds outside the palace, protecting him from the protesters who cried "Heretic!" and from his jubilant followers, who were crowding to be near him. Illuminated by the flames of the torches that lit the room, a stack of books could be seen at the foot of the emperor's throne.

Luther slowly approached the pile of books. He could barely see their titles in the gathering dusk, yet he knew every word between their covers. The books were his own work, and the teachings that they contained were so critical of the Roman Catholic church that he had already been condemned by the pope as a heretic (a dissenter from established Church doctrine). Outlawed by the spiritual authorities, the young professor had been summoned to defend his position before the secular, or civil,

Elected Holy Roman emperor in 1519, Charles V had little success in his endeavors to establish effective government within his vast domains. He spent much of his reign directing the defense of his empire's borders and countering the intrigues of his nobles.

Martin Luther (left, in monk's habit; 1483—1546) defends his criticisms of the Roman Catholic church before Holy Roman Emperor Charles V (seated at right, wearing crown; 1500—1558) at a conference convened by Charles in Worms, Germany, April 17, 1521. Luther's defiant stand marked the beginning of the period of religious upheaval known as the Reformation.

authorities. Luther knew that the emperor was now his last line of defense against the wrath of the Church. If Charles V were to condemn him as well, his life would be in great danger.

It was due to the fact that he was a friar, or member of a religious order whose work is conducted within society at large, that Luther had been at liberty to take his teachings out into the world. His teachings, now the subject of immense controversy, might never have become widely known had the young man been a monk—confined to the monastery and leading a life of contemplation. It was a friar's traditional freedom to preach in public, to teach at universities, and to move from one monastery to another, that had made the world beyond the walls of the cloister Luther's forum for discussion and the development of new ideas.

As Luther drew close to the emperor and his entourage, the crowd grew silent. At Charles's signal, Johann von Eck, chancellor to the archbishop of Trier, read aloud the titles of the books: "*To the Christian Nobility of the German Nation Concerning the Reform of the Christian Estate . . . The Freedom of a Christian Man. . . .*" Luther gazed into the large diamond at the emperor's throat. In its brilliance he imagined he saw the many fires that had already consumed hundreds of his books in town squares throughout Germany. Even when he closed his eyes the vision lingered, and it seemed to him that he could hear the crackling roar of the blaze. Anger began to well up inside him, and perspiration trickled from his brow.

"Luther!" shouted von Eck. "His Highness the Emperor wishes to know if you are the author of these books." The young friar replied, "The books are all mine, and I have written more." The official then asked, "Do you defend them all, or do you care to reject a part?" The friar bowed his head for a moment. He then asked that he be allowed time in which to consider his answer, because, he said, "this is a question of faith and the salvation of souls." The emperor, himself a devout man and in no mood to have such an important dispute brought to a hurried conclusion, agreed to Luther's request.

> *A single friar [Martin Luther] errs in his opinion which is against all of Christendom and according to which all of Christianity will be and will always have been in error both in the past thousand years and even more in the present. . . . I am determined to proceed against him as a notorious heretic.*
>
> —HOLY ROMAN EMPEROR CHARLES V
> in his condemnation of Luther, issued at the Diet of Worms, April 19, 1521

The young professor was allowed 24 hours in which to prepare a final statement.

At 6:00 P.M. on the following day, in front of Emperor Charles V and his court, Martin Luther gave a 10-minute speech in Latin and then repeated it in German. "I cannot," he declared, "renounce these works . . . without increasing tyranny and impiety. . . . If I am shown my error, I will be the first to throw my books into the fire. I have been reminded of the dissensions which my teaching engenders. I can answer only in the words of the Lord, 'I came not to bring peace, but a sword!'"

When he had finished speaking, Luther looked back over his shoulder and saw a teeming crowd pressing through the great doors of the hall to hear the emperor's response. Charles V, however, had not come to Worms to enter into a theological, or religious, debate with the rebellious friar whose teachings had captured the imagination of the German people and were now threatening to disturb the peace of his domains. The emperor felt that he had no alternative but to reject Luther's statement.

"Answer simply, Luther," said von Eck. "Will you or will you not retract all that you have written?" Unhesitatingly, Luther replied, "I cannot and will not retract anything, for it is neither safe nor right to act against one's conscience. Here I stand! I cannot do otherwise. God help me! Amen."

The crowd was in an uproar. Rising from his seat, von Eck shook his fist at the departing Luther, and told the young friar that the issues at stake were far more important than the dictates of one man's conscience. Luther walked from the palace and into the throngs of waiting townspeople. Again, shouts of "Heretic!" assailed him from all sides.

Martin Luther had never intended to disturb the prevailing social order or to earn the hatred and enmity of the leaders of the Roman Catholic church. He simply wanted to debate the abuses of its power of which he believed the Church to be guilty. But suddenly thousands of Germans were buying his books; suddenly he had a substantial audience that was eager to hear his proposals for reforming the Church and his revolutionary views on such im-

*And while I slept or drank Wittenberg beer with my friends, the Word of God so greatly weakened the papacy that no prince or emperor ever inflicted such losses upon it. I did nothing. The Word did everything.*
—MARTIN LUTHER

portant subjects as freedom from sin, faith in God, and the role of the Church. Luther was now emerging as the head of a movement that would eventually divide the Christian world community and dramatically change the course of history.

The history of the period reveals that Germany was ripe for a reformer like Luther. Luther's Germany was a part of the Holy Roman Empire, a vast tract of western and central European territory covering much of present-day Austria, Belgium, Czechoslovakia, Germany, eastern France, the Netherlands, and northern Italy. During Luther's time the Holy Roman Empire, while still an important political entity, was not as powerful or as united as it had been several centuries earlier. It is in the context of the condition of the empire that Luther's audience with Charles V is best understood.

The first Holy Roman Empire had been established in A.D. 800, when Charles the Great (who is also known as Charlemagne), king of the Franks, was crowned emperor by Pope Leo III. Prior to his coronation, Charles had annexed much territory in northern Italy and central Europe.

Following the death of the Holy Roman Emperor Charles III in 880, the empire that had been founded by Charles the Great was gradually overwhelmed by barbarian invaders from eastern Europe. When the eastern branch of Charles the Great's dynasty died out early in the 10th century, the people of the empire's Germanic provinces revived their ancient practice of electing a monarch. In 962 King Otto the Great of Germany was crowned emperor of Rome by Pope John XII. Though Otto's empire was confined to Italy and Germany, he intended that it should eventually embrace all of western Europe. Frederick I Barbarossa, who became Holy Roman emperor in 1155, believed that the empire was established by God and that it was as important an institution as the Roman Catholic church.

Barbarossa's successor, Frederick II, attempted to emulate Frederick I by seeking to make the empire the greatest secular power in Europe. However, he met with little success, mainly because the popes regarded the empire as a threat to the influence of the Church. By 1273, when Rudolf of Habsburg was elected to the imperial throne, the empire was already in decline.

During the more than 500 years that had passed since Otto's coronation, the Holy Roman emperors had been forced to fight on two fronts in their efforts to retain their political supremacy—against the princes and dukes of Germany on the one hand, and against the popes on the other.

The emperors' power and influence had begun to deteriorate particularly fast from the 14th century onward, when the expansion of commerce and the resulting concentration of wealth in the fast-growing cities meant that German society was no longer predominantly based upon agriculture and had thus ceased to be the kind of society over which the Holy Roman emperors had originally held sway. The failure of the emperors to gain the support of the

Dating from the 12th century, the cathedral at Worms is one of the finest examples of Romanesque architecture in all Europe. It was near this site that Luther defended his beliefs before Charles V in 1521, answering questions put to him on the emperor's behalf by Johann von Eck, an official in the service of the archbishop of Trier.

A map shows the political divisions of Europe during the early 16th century. The Holy Roman Empire, first established by Charles the Great, king of the Franks (A.D. 742–814), in 800, had been wracked by barbarian invasions and internal conflict for several centuries when Charles V became emperor in June 1519.

urban middle class also contributed to their decline. At the same time, many of the powers previously enjoyed by the emperors passed to the princes and dukes who ruled the many small states into which Germany was then divided. Moreover, the seven very powerful princes who chose the emperor tended to favor the weakest candidate. These princes, who were known as electors, had no wish to appoint a ruler who might seek to curtail their power and privileges. Charles V's predecessor, Maximilian I, was the last Holy Roman emperor to have attempted to strengthen his position. Following Charles V's accession to the imperial throne, political power in

Germany became decentralized, divided among the German princes.

Charles V had inherited a huge international regime, with many commitments outside of Germany. His armies were fighting the French on the empire's western borders and the Turks in southern Europe and the eastern Mediterranean. Any imperial attempt to stop a mass uprising at home, therefore, usually proved to have been either inadequate or belated. Since the emperor was generally preoccupied with matters of foreign policy, Germany's princes were willing to support controversial people like Luther if doing so seemed likely to enhance their own positions. In short, the political situation inside Germany was so uncertain that figures like Lu-

Entitled *Flemish Country Festival*, this painting by the great Flemish artist Pieter Brueghel the Younger (1564—1638) offers an idyllic view of peasant life in Europe during the 16th century. It was upon the peasants of Germany that Luther's teachings had their greatest initial impact.

ther could attract a large following before the central government resorted to suppression.

German society was also in a state of unrest. The great mass of poor people in the small cities and villages resented the repressive policies of the wealthy and powerful nobles. Many free peasants were losing their smallholdings and becoming serfs—laborers without rights. As serfs, they were forced to work on the estates of the nobles; they were forbidden to hunt or fish; and they were heavily taxed on the produce that they grew. It was in this social environment that Luther sought to bring about a renewed awareness of the personal freedom that he considered the birthright of all Christians. The peasants, who lived in fear of landlords, tax collectors, and churchmen who preached that God was unloving and merciless, found a message of hope and strength in Luther's teachings.

The religious climate too was extremely unsettled at that time. The Church was in turmoil and plagued by corruption. The Church exerted tremendous power and influence over the lives of German Christians. In fact, Christianity was the most widespread intellectual and spiritual influence in Europe at the time. While the Orthodox church was a strong force in eastern Europe, the Roman Catholic church was not only the sole religious institution of western Europe but was also the wealthiest and the most powerful.

At that time, the Roman Catholic church operated in much the same way as a business corporation does nowadays. The Church owned almost a third of all the land in the Holy Roman Empire. In some areas a fourth of all business property was held by the Church. The Church imposed an annual levy, known as "Peter's pence," on every household in Christendom. In addition to this tax, every Catholic was supposed to pay the Church a *tithe*, a tax amounting to 10 percent of his or her income and which was used to support the local parish church. The revenues from these sources had made the Catholic church extremely rich. With power and prosperity, however, came decadence and disrepute.

> *A cobbler, a smith, a farmer, each has the work and office of his trade . . . and everyone by means of his own work or office must benefit and serve every other, that in this way many kinds of work may be done for the bodily and spiritual welfare of the community, even as all the members of the body serve one another.*
>
> —MARTIN LUTHER

Luther called Rome, the home of the pope, "the dwelling place of dragons, specters, and witches." Many Catholics were disturbed by the avarice and immorality of the popes, cardinals, and other high-ranking churchmen. Ecclesiastical appointments were often sold for huge amounts of money. Some clergymen would buy numerous positions and thus control vast revenues. Many bishops were also princes, and cardinals enjoyed the same position as princes in the social hierarchy. Some senior churchmen held three sees, or regional appointments, and yet failed to perform their duties in any of them. Several recent popes had become notorious for their corruption. Unlike the popes of today, the pontiffs

*The Beggars*, **by the Flemish artist Pieter Brueghel the Elder (c. 1525–1569), whose work portrayed the lives of the lower orders in 16th-century Europe with great vividness. Some historians feel that much of the destitution prevailing in Germany during Luther's time was directly attributable to the policies of the Catholic church.**

ALINARI/ART RESOURCE

As head of the Catholic church from 1492 to 1503, Pope Alexander VI (1431–1503) became notorious for corruption and immorality. He greatly encouraged the sale of indulgences as a method of generating revenue for the Church.

of Luther's time sent armies into battle, hunted game, and generally neglected their religious duties in favor of worldly pleasures. The moral corruption of the clergy was particularly pronounced. Some historians estimate that almost a third of all clergymen had mistresses. Though some Church leaders felt that clergymen should be allowed to marry, the majority did not. Priests were regularly fined by the Church for keeping women and fathering illegitimate children. Most senior churchmen felt that permitting priests to marry would have deprived the Church of a valuable source of income.

Faced with this situation, many people had begun to feel that the Church was in need of reform. However, previous reformers had met with fierce opposition from the religious establishment. Only a strong, charismatic leader with a large following could hope to succeed.

Despite the worldly ways of the churchmen, the Germans were, on the whole, a people of faith—a faith that was seasoned with superstitions derived from German folklore. Though willing to believe the teachings of the Catholic church, the people were disenchanted with the profiteering and depravity of the clergy. One form of ecclesiastical avarice, which Luther attacked with particular vehemence during his earliest years as a reformer, was the practice of selling indulgences—letters issued by the pope that purported to guarantee the forgiveness of sins.

An indulgence was basically a transfer of credit. At that time, the Church taught that God's son, Jesus Christ; Christ's mother, the Virgin Mary; and all the saints were better than they needed to be to earn spiritual salvation. The excess of merit that these holy figures had acquired was regarded as infinite in the case of Christ, whom Catholics believe to be both part of God and entirely free of sin. These excess merits were viewed as a kind of treasury that could be drawn upon by sinners so as to improve their spiritual "solvency."

The selling of indulgences had become especially widespread after 1476, when Pope Sixtus IV announced that indulgences could shorten the amount of time that a sinner would have to spend in purgatory—the place of punishment where, according to Catholic doctrine, the dead make atonement for their sins. This particular papal pronouncement had encouraged believers to purchase indulgences both for themselves (to shorten their future sentence) and for their dead loved ones.

Sixtus IV's eagerness to promote indulgences was one of the first great examples of the extent to which the Church had begun to reflect the ideals generated during during the cultural period known as the Renaissance. (This is a French term that means rebirth.) Originating in Italy and characterized by a revival of interest in the literature, philosophy, and politics of ancient Greece and Rome, the Renaissance gave rise to new forms of consciousness. One of these forms of consciousness was known as humanism. Developed independently of Catholic teachings by Italian intellectuals during the 14th and 15th centuries, humanism was eventually to influence all Europe. Its adherents viewed the world in strictly human terms. Humanism represented a radical departure from medieval ways of thinking,

> *Make way for the true servant of God, Doctor Luther, to preach God's word. He has guided thousands of people to Jesus Christ, the true fountain from which every thirsty person may drink all that he desires.*
> —HARTMUTH VON CRONBERG
> German knight,
> writing in 1520

The magnificent interior of St. Peter's Basilica in Rome is but one example of the many grandiose works of architecture that the Catholic church commissioned during the 16th century. Luther considered such projects a waste of money, claiming that they were being built "with the skin, flesh, and bones" of ordinary believers.

which had viewed the world exclusively in relation to God.

The relationship between humanism and the Church was uneasy. Many churchmen distrusted the humanists because they concerned themselves with the study of pre-Christian, pagan cultures. However, despite the fact that humanism and Catholicism were essentially incompatible, there was to be no open conflict between them. This was because the popes took a leading role as patrons of the new learning. Sixtus IV, who devoted most of his time to financing art projects and striking devious and unprincipled political bargains, was a typical Renaissance despot. Alexander VI, who reigned from 1492 to 1503, was a spectacularly immoral pontiff who is still regarded by Catholic historians as a disgrace to the papacy. Leo X, who reigned from 1513 to 1521, spent more money on parades and gambling than he did on either the Church or the arts. The assault upon the papacy, which Luther was initiating by taking a stand before Emperor Charles V, was directed against an institution that possessed very little of the moral and spiritual authority that it had known several centuries earlier.

Many papal letters of indulgence took the process even further than had Sixtus IV's, promising complete forgiveness of sins rather than merely a reduction in the penalty for having committed them. The fact that the Church was making vast amounts of money from the gullibility of ordinary believers greatly disturbed Luther, who had expressed the opinion that Rome was being built "out of the blood and hide" of the faithful. The fact that the Renaissance popes had reduced Christianity to a commercial undertaking was ultimately to cost the papacy a substantial proportion of its credibility. Because it had hardly been touched by the Renaissance, Luther's Germany was still a bastion of sincere religious belief. And it was this personal sincerity of conviction that enabled Luther to take his stand before Charles V and not to back down for fear of the possible consequences. Luther had refused to go against his conscience, even if it meant that he might be burned at the stake.

Though Charles V was officially to condemn Luther just five weeks after their encounter in the bishop's palace at Worms, Luther would survive the emperor's wrath. Several German nobles who disagreed with Charles's decision would take steps to ensure that Luther came to no harm. Thus, the open and and public defiance of the Church that Luther displayed before Charles V would prove to have been but one of the earliest instances of confrontation in a life devoted to questioning the established order.

The stand that Luther took that day marked the beginning of the period of religious, political, and social upheaval known as the Reformation. As a result of Luther's attack on those aspects of Catholicism that he considered no part of God's purpose for Christians, Christendom would find itself divided. Never again would it know the unity that had characterized the first 1,500 years of its existence. A new, non-Catholic form of Christianity would be erected upon the foundations that Luther had laid, a form of Christianity whose very name would reflect its dissenting nature—Protestantism. The story of the man whose example inspired these great changes began 38 years before the confrontation at Worms, in a village in the German province of Hesse.

A contemporary print portrays the sale of indulgences to the faithful during the 16th century. In guaranteeing Catholics absolution from their sins by the purchase of indulgences, the Church was able to fill its coffers to overflowing.

# 2

# The Convert

The evening of November 10, 1483, was no more eventful than any other in the small Thuringian mountain village of Eisleben. Peasants, done with their day's work, walked home to suppers of oatbread, sauerkraut, and mugs of whey. A miner named Hans Luther strode through the narrow streets, his hooded cape flapping about him in the wind. "Perhaps the Lord will see fit to give me a son today!" he said to himself.

As Hans entered his cottage, his wife, Margarethe Luther, called out to him: "Hans, come quickly!" The stocky German miner climbed the stairs two at a time, the wooden boards creaking beneath his weight. Though Hans was tired, his fatigue was as nothing compared to the joy that he felt knowing that his wife was about to bear him a child. The Luthers were poor, but Hans had hopes of a successful future in the copper mines of nearby Mansfeld. He wanted a better life for his child than the one that he had known.

Later that night Margarethe Luther gave birth to a son. On the following morning, the boy was baptized. It was St. Martin's Day. About a year later the Luthers moved to Mansfeld, where Hans set about improving the family's fortunes.

Like her husband, Hans, Margarethe Luther was a strict disciplinarian who sometimes beat her son mercilessly. The young Luther's perception of God as an angry, judgmental figure undoubtedly had much to do with the severity of his upbringing.

*The Village School*, a painting by Dutch artist Jan Steen (c. 1626–1679). Luther's experiences during the early years of his education later prompted him to write: "The schoolmasters in my days were tyrants and executioners; the schools were jails and hells! And in spite of fear and misery, floggings and tremblings, nothing was learned!"

Martin Luther's father, Hans Luther, as portrayed by German artist Lucas Cranach (1472–1553). Originally a miner, Hans Luther eventually became the owner of several small foundries. His improved position provided him with sufficient income to send young Martin to school.

At first, life was not easy for the Luthers in their new home. It was to be several years before Hans achieved prosperity. As a result, Martin began to help his mother with the strenuous household tasks just as soon as he was old enough. Margarethe would don her long cloak and take Martin deep into the forest to gather firewood. As the two plodded home, Margarethe would tell her son folktales, scaring him with stories of witches and phantoms, of demons drawing down the moon and riding through the air on the backs of black cows. "Six witches were broken on the wheel; four were crushed limb by limb with an iron bar blessed by the pope!" Martin's eyes widened as he listened to his mother's descriptions of the kinds of revenge that God's servants were known to take against the unholy. "If a soul forgets to pay tithes to the church, dear Martin, their soul will know no rest. Neither going to Mass nor regular prayers can protect you! Fear God, my son! Lightning bolts and the plague await those who wander into the dark forest of sin. St. Anne protect us!" (St. Anne, the patron saint of miners, was often called upon in the Luther household. At the mention of her name, both Margarethe and young Martin would make the sign of the cross, Martin's hand shaking as his imagination conjured up visions of the flames of hell.)

Hans and Margarethe were very stern with their son. Years later Luther would recall that "my father once whipped me so that I ran away and felt ugly toward him until he was at pains to win me back. . . . My mother once beat me until the blood flowed, for having stolen a miserable nut."

The situation was no different at the first school that Martin attended. A senior pupil known as the *lupus*, or wolf, would pace up and down between the rows of desks, listening for anyone not speaking in Latin, the ancient language that they were there to learn. The *lupus* would report the misbehavers to the teachers, who would administer beatings at the end of each week. "The schoolmasters in my days," Luther would later write, "were tyrants and executioners; the schools were jails and hells! And in spite of fear and misery, floggings and tremblings, nothing was learned!" Luther would also declare that the grammar tests given to the young scholars had been "nothing short of torture." He came to form strong opinions on how to improve teaching: "Whatever the method that is used, it ought to pay attention to the differences in aptitude and teach in such a way that all children are treated with equal love."

The strict regime of correction and punishment to which Luther was subjected by his parents and his teachers was mirrored in what they taught him about God. The young boy came to see God as an angry, judgmental figure. He saw himself as a sinful, feeble creature scampering to do just the right thing to please his superiors—his parents, his teachers, and God. It is perhaps because he was so desperately eager to gain the approval of his elders that Luther proved to be an extremely successful student. Not only was he bright and enthusiastic, but he managed to maintain his devotion to his studies despite the fact that he suffered from occasional bouts of depression, a condition that would plague him for the rest of his life. Even during his boyhood, Luther's feelings of happiness were overshadowed by the question that was always to preoccupy him: "How can one lead a perfect life before God?"

> *God uses lust to impel man to marriage, ambition to office, avarice to earning, and fear to faith.*
> —MARTIN LUTHER

It was at his next school that Luther began to see an answer. In 1496, at age 12, Luther entered the cathedral school at Magdeburg, where several of the teachers were members of a religious order called the Brethren of the Common Life. There, the young Luther gained his exposure to people who had dedicated their lives to God. Like other friars, the Brethren of the Common Life took vows of poverty, chastity, and obedience. Martin was impressed by their quiet and contemplative piety. He became even more fascinated with the commonly held belief that the monastic way of life was a route to perfection when, one day, he beheld a Franciscan friar begging in the streets. The elderly friar seemed to Martin "the picture of death, mere skin and bones." When he was informed that the aged ascetic was a duke who had forsaken his riches in order to devote himself to the holy life, Martin felt the first stirrings of a desire to enter a religious community.

Martin excelled in writing and in rhetoric (the art of making speeches) while he was in Magdeburg, and it seemed that he was well on his way to becoming a successful lawyer. In 1498 Hans Luther moved his son to a school in Eisenach, where he stayed for two years.

Even though the teachers at his new school were not directing him toward the monastic life, Luther did not forget his experiences in Magdeburg. The education that Luther received at Eisenach was designed to prepare students for civic life. The school's headmaster would always, as he entered the classroom, remove his hat as a mark of respect to his pupils. He fervently believed that God might intend many of them to become important public figures.

Though Luther wanted to fulfill his father's and his headmaster's dreams for his future, it was at this time that he began to experience serious inner

> *I was imbued with noxious ideas from boyhood, so that I would be terrified and grow pale at even the mention of Christ's name, because I was persuaded that he was a judge.*
> —MARTIN LUTHER
> writing in 1535

**Hell, a painting by Dutch artist Dirck Bouts (1400–1475). Luther, like most Catholics of his day, was brought up to believe that torments such as those depicted by Bouts would be visited upon all sinners after they died.**

**Luther vows to become a monk. While returning to Erfurt in July 1505, Luther was thrown to the ground when a lightning bolt struck beside him. Terrified, he vowed to become a monk and entered the Order of Augustinian Eremites two weeks later.**

conflict, a struggle with his conscience that became ever greater as he prepared to enter the university. Should he be a great magistrate, or should he follow his conscience and lead a life of holiness, setting himself apart from the world? Would he ever be happy, he wondered, if he chose not to pursue his desire to serve God wholeheartedly?

Luther enrolled at the University of Erfurt in May 1501, at age 17, and commenced upon the long course of preliminary studies that aspiring law students were obliged to take in order to qualify for admission to law school. At that time the university, which was more than 100 years old, had 2,000 students. It enjoyed an outstanding reputation for academic excellence. Luther studied Latin, logic, philosophy, astronomy, music, arithmetic, geometry, and theology. Discipline was as strict as it had been at Magdeburg and Eisenach. The students were awakened at 4:00 A.M. Lectures began as the sun rose and continued until 5:00 P.M. The first meal of the day was taken at 10:00 A.M. The students hurried from class to class, pausing only for the briefest of conversations before the next lecture commenced, whispering quietly to each other in the required Latin.

Luther gained his Bachelor's degree in September

1502 and his Master's degree in January 1505. Possession of these qualifications meant that he was now entitled to register for a law course, which he did in May of that same year.

On the evening of July 2, 1505, while walking back to Erfurt after a visit to his parents, Luther was deep in thought, still tormented by the inner struggle between his desire to fulfill his parents' dreams and his burgeoning interest in the prospect of devoting his life to God. He wanted to please his parents, yet their hopes for him differed greatly from his own ambitions.

When Luther was barely half a mile from the gates of the city, the skies darkened and a summer storm erupted. Suddenly, a bolt of lightning struck beside him and he was thrown to the ground. According to his own account, Luther felt, at the moment of cataclysm, as if "walled around with the terror and horror of sudden death."

In his book *Here I Stand: A Life of Martin Luther*, historian and theologian Roland H. Bainton describes Luther's revelation thus: "In that single flash [Luther] saw the denouement of the drama of existence. There was God the all-terrible, Christ the inexorable, and all the leering fiends springing from their lurking places in pond and wood . . . that they might seize his shock of curly hair and bolt him into hell."

On rising, Luther called out in fright and desperation, "St. Anne help me! I will become a monk!" He could no longer follow his father's wishes.

On July 17, 1505, Luther walked through the streets of Erfurt to the monastery where he would don the black habit, or robe, of the Order of Augustinian Eremites. Nothing in the demeanor of the young student who entered the gates of the cloister that day would have suggested to the prior of the monastery that here was a man who would be utterly transformed by the way of life upon which he was embarking. Martin Luther, the earnest scholar who declared that he was in need of God's grace and the prior's mercy, would one day cause unprecedented discord within the church to which he was so eager to give his absolute obedience.

# 3

# The Novice

At the time of his entry into the friary, Luther was, by his own account, overwhelmed by the presence of sin in his life and much preoccupied with the prospect of the punishment that he believed lay waiting for him after death. In the friary, Luther could devote himself entirely to earning salvation by living a life of discipline, self-denial, and piety. He did not enter the cloister intending to change the world or to challenge the Catholic church. On the contrary, he felt that by leaving the world far behind him and obeying Church doctrine to the letter he could ensure that he would be admitted to heaven when he died.

The reformed Order of Augustinian Eremites was the strictest in Erfurt. Unlike the members of the older orders, who remained in the same monastery all their lives, living by the 6th-century A.D. Rule of St. Benedict (which required that its adherents spend much time in contemplation) the reformed orders were committed to "passing on the fruits of contemplation" by working in society. The Augustinian Eremites were also known as an "observant" order, which meant that they had recently adopted a stricter regime than had previously been customary.

After spending a few weeks as a postulant, during which time the senior friars kept him under obser-

A silver chalice dating from the 15th century. Although the life of a monk in Luther's time was simple and austere, its accoutrements were generally opulent and ornate. Painstaking workmanship and precious metals were combined to create religious artifacts of great beauty.

As a young friar, Luther gained the respect of his colleagues and superiors for his academic brilliance, his oratorical skills, and his spirituality. At this point in his career there was little to indicate that he would eventually be outlawed by the Catholic authorities for his outspoken criticism of their policies.

vation and considered his suitability for entry into the order, Luther was formally admitted to the novitiate. As a novice, Luther would live as a member of the order for a period of one year. At the end of that time, his superiors would decide whether or not he should remain at the cloister.

The rules of the cloister were severe, but young Luther found much solace in the regular rhythms of the monastic existence, which he viewed as a purposive and inspirational change from the uncertainties and distractions of the world that he had forsaken. Every day, Luther and the other friars rose at 2:00 A.M., donned their robes, and silently filed into the chapel for the first of the seven periods set aside for communal prayer. Regular fasting was a feature of life at the friary, but Martin would often exceed the formal requirements. Describing this period of his life, Luther wrote: "If ever a monk got to heaven by his monkery, it was I. . . . If I had kept on any longer, I should have killed myself with vigils, prayers, reading, and other work." According to the other friars, Luther fasted so often that he came to look emaciated. None of this, however, brought him the peace for which he yearned. "When I looked for Christ," he said, "it seemed to me as if I saw the Devil."

Though Luther had assumed the external attributes of the holy life—the monk's cowl, the shaven head—and was diligently following the strict regime of fasting and prayer, he was deeply disturbed by what he saw as the failure of his inner life. Feeling incapable of cleansing himself of sin, Luther became increasingly troubled by guilt. It is probable that even at this early stage of his career Luther was haunted by the suspicion that he had set himself an impossible task. This sensation of inadequacy

St. Augustine (354—430) in his chambers. The religious order to which Luther belonged—the Augustinian Eremites—derived its name and its precepts from this great philosopher and churchman. While Luther found Augustine's theological treatises inspiring, he doubted that the Augustinians' extreme asceticism and self-denial could truly bring a man closer to God.

**On several occasions during his early years with the Augustinians, Luther collapsed from constant fasting and studying. He later wrote: "If I had kept on any longer, I should have killed myself with vigils, prayers, reading, and other work."**

was to be much in evidence in his later writings: "This word [by which he meant the teachings of Jesus] is too high and hard that anyone should fulfill it. This is proved, not merely by our Lord's word, but by our own experience and feeling. Take any upright man. . . . He will get along very nicely with those who do not provoke him, but let someone proffer only the slightest irritation and he will flare up in anger . . . if not against friends, then against enemies. Flesh and blood cannot rise above it."

The Augustinian Eremites believed that through constant prayer, meditation, and self-denial they could live their lives in a manner pleasing to God. However, the harder Luther tried, the more he came to believe that "flesh and blood cannot rise above" the human capacity for sinfulness that separates man from God.

At times, however, Luther felt elated, as if he were "among choirs of angels," particularly when he read the works of St. Augustine. The young friar would fill the margins of his books with comments and questions. Luther's annotations make it clear that he was especially impressed by the 5th-century theologian's mysticism—by his insights into God's nature. Above all else Luther devoted himself to the study of the Bible, learning much of it by heart. His superiors began to perceive that Luther possessed a first-rate intellect.

Luther made his full profession of vows in the summer of 1506 and was admitted into the Augustinian community. He then began to train for the priesthood. Luther had to learn every detail of the actions to be performed by the priest during the ceremony known as the Mass, as well as every word of the text that the priest had to recite during the proceedings. Following his ordination, which took place on April 3, 1507, Luther began to apply himself even harder to learning the intricacies of the Mass. He was painfully aware of the fact that making even the slightest mistake in leading the Mass was considered a major sin.

On Sunday morning, May 2, 1507, the newly ordained Luther prepared to celebrate, or perform, his first Mass. He carefully draped himself with the appropriate cowl; he spent the morning meditating and fasting in his cell. Before God, his peers, and his family (Hans and Margarethe were coming; he had not seen them since his university days), he would offer up the bread and wine, bless them, and witness the "miracle" of transubstantiation—the process whereby, according to Catholic doctrine, the bread and wine become the body and blood of Christ. This would be his role as an ordained Catholic priest. This is what he had been longing for— and fearing. His nervousness at the prospect of seeing his father, who had never forgiven him for quitting his legal career, was as nothing compared to the anxiety that he felt about celebrating Mass correctly.

The ceremony began. Luther repeated the words that were now so familiar to him. He took the silver chalice filled with wine and raised it up before the altar. "We offer unto Thee, the living, the true, the eternal God. . . ." He paused. Suddenly he felt as if he were going to faint. Here was the miracle of transubstantiation. Luther felt so humbled by the significance of the ceremony that he was unable to continue.

"Who am I," prayed Luther, "that I should lift up mine eyes or raise my hands to the divine Majesty? The angels surround Him! At His nod the earth trembles." The chalice began to shake. Luther could not control his fear; his knees were buckling. He turned to the prior, who was at his side assisting with the Mass. Familiar with the difficulties that new celebrants sometimes faced, the prior brought Luther back to his task.

For Luther, the experience of celebrating his first Mass had been traumatic. He later used the word *Anfechtung* (a sensation of loneliness, disbelief, and despair) to describe what he had felt at the moment of crisis. Though his greatest desire was to know and serve God, Luther had suddenly become convinced that he was not worthy to say God's name, let alone celebrate the miracle of the Mass. Luther recalled, "When I came to the words 'Thee, most merciful Father,' the thought that I had to speak to God without a mediator almost made me flee. . . ." Though Luther finished the Mass and would go on to perform others, something crucial had happened.

In his book *Luther: A Life*, historian John M. Todd comments that Luther's "anguished internal cry, only marginally visible externally, was the first note of a theme which he was to orchestrate vastly in later years. The revolution he started was precisely about the matter of how man is to manage his relationship with that which men call God."

Luther's first Mass was critical to his development as a truly revolutionary theologian. It represented his first uncertain but resounding step in a new direction, along a path of intellectual and religious inquiry that would lead him inexorably toward a new theological landscape, a landscape that was to be revealed by the transformation of belief.

*Though I lived as a monk without reproach, I felt that I was a sinner before God. . . . I could not believe that he was placated by my satisfaction. I did not love, yes, I hated the righteous God who punishes sinners, and secretly, if not blasphemously. . . . I was angry with God.*

— MARTIN LUTHER
writing in 1546 of the depression that plagued him during his first years as a monk

Monastic life during Luther's time was particularly severe. Much of a monk's day, which started at 2:00 A.M.
and continued until nightfall, was taken up with periods
of prayer and meditation. This extreme austerity stood
in great contrast to the luxuriant and indulgent lifestyle
enjoyed by the leaders of the Church.

Auril.

| | | | |
|---|---|---|---|
| | | g | S aint valer |
| .x. | | A ꝛ. | l egypuenne |
| xix. | | b ꝛ. | S. pancace |
| viij. | | c ꝛ. | S. ambꝛoise |
| | | d ꝛ. | S aint yꝛaine |
| xvi. | | e ꝛ. | S. tymothe |
| v. | | f ꝛ. | S. machaire |
| | | g id. | S. apollinaire |
| xiiij. | | A id. | S aint pꝛoꝛ |
| .ij. | | b id. | S aint pꝛofixt |
| | | c id. | S aint leon |
| .x. | | d id. | S aint marcel |
| | | e id. | S. ualeuen |
| xviij. | | f id. | S aint eufeme |
| vij. | | g id. | S aint pꝛine |

# 4

# The Pilgrim

Luther plunged back into his studies with all the devotion of a man desperately in need of the certainties that the routine of religious life provided. His superiors decided that he should begin to work toward his *Baccalaureus Biblicus*, or Bible degree. The course of study for this degree normally took five years, at the end of which time Luther would be qualified to lecture on the Bible. (His Master's degree only qualified him to teach philosophy.)

Inasmuch as the Baccalaureus Biblicus was a major qualification, Luther's superiors would never have proposed him for the course unless they had been entirely convinced that he would prove more than equal to the demands that it would make upon his intellectual abilities. A scholar in possession of this qualification would automatically proceed to the two-year course of study leading to the degree known as *Sententiarius*, which would qualify him to give lectures on the *Sentences*, an enormous and extremely important collection of religious texts that had been compiled in the 12th century by a theologian named Peter Lombard. A scholar who had been designated Sententiarius stood a good chance of being selected to take a Doctorate in theology—the highest qualification a theologian could hope to gain.

Luther's remarkable intellectual abilities gained him quick promotions from the outset of his academic career. In 1512, at age 28, he was encouraged to take his doctorate in theology—a qualification that most scholars of the period rarely achieved until they were 40 years of age or older.

A 15th-century manuscript depicts members of the French nobility on a pilgrimage to Rome. In 1510 Luther made such a pilgrimage himself, but with none of the ceremony suggested here. Ironically, it was while he was in Rome that Luther began to doubt the legitimacy of papal authority.

Luther soon began to find the combination of studying at the university and at the cloister very taxing. In compliance with the Augustinians' strict rules of observance, any scholar who missed one of the community's several daily prayer sessions because he had to give a lecture at the university was obliged to recite the order of service on his own time. However, despite this imposition, Luther drew upon his ever-expanding reserves of willpower and piety, successfully meeting all the demands that his hectic career was making upon him. Though still occasionally plagued by sensations of *Anfechtung*, he refused to let such feelings interfere with his work. Luther's superiors considered his devotion to study and correct observance exceptional, and his speaking ability outstanding.

In the fall of 1508 Luther's efforts earned him a substantial promotion. During his frequent visits to Erfurt, the superior of the reformed Augustinian houses, Dr. Johann von Staupitz, had been informed of Luther's remarkable academic progress. As a result, von Staupitz, who was also professor of Bible studies at the recently founded University of Wittenberg, became convinced that Luther would be a valuable addition to the university staff. He therefore requested that Luther be allowed to come to Wittenberg to lecture on philosophy.

Luther spent a year in Wittenberg, and did so well that he was awarded his Baccalaureus Biblicus on March 9, 1509, after just two years of study. He greatly enjoyed the challenges of his new position, and found the combination of lecturing on philosophy and continuing with his own studies in theology difficult but rewarding. Von Staupitz followed Luther's progress with much interest, and it soon became apparent that he had great hopes for him. Von Staupitz was finding it increasingly hard to fulfill his commitments as both senior lecturer in Bible study and vicar of the reformed Augustinian order, which maintained many friaries throughout Germany. In the fall of 1509, just as von Staupitz had become more convinced than ever that Luther should take over his position at Wittenberg, the prior of the Erfurt community requested that Luther return there to teach at the cloister.

Upon his return to Erfurt, Luther qualified as Sententiarius and began to lecture on theology. He immersed himself in the writings of St. Augustine, paying particular attention to his monumental treatise *The City of God*. Luther also began to study Peter Lombard's *Sentences* in greater detail. In the notes that Luther made in the margins of these texts there is one phrase that appears with great frequency—*coram deo*, which is Latin for "in God's presence." In his biography of Luther, Todd proposes that the repeated use of this phrase indicates that Luther possessed an "intense, personal and vibrant piety." This, combined with Luther's emerging dislike of abstract philosophical statements and his increasing tendency to view life as a *fluxus*, or flow of events, rather than an unchangeable condition, was largely in accord with Catholic tradition. Any doubts that assailed him during this period of his life had more to do with his capacity for self-criticism than with the state of the Roman Catholic church.

In the fall of 1510 Luther accompanied one of the senior friars on a special mission to Rome. The Augustinian cloisters were in dispute over administrative matters, and the issue could only be resolved

**The Wittenberg Castle church, where Luther often preached. In his sermons, which were often based on lectures he had given at the University of Wittenberg, Luther employed language of startling, almost brutal intensity, often holding his audience spellbound.**

by a papal decision. The journey, which was made on foot, took seven weeks. The two friars trudged over the high Tyrolean pass in the Bavarian mountains, along the shores of Lake Como, and south through Italy. When they reached the city of Milan, they stopped to see the magnificent cathedral that was being constructed there. They traveled through the Tuscan mountains to Florence, where they saw the great palaces of the ruling de Medici dynasty and the town square where, when Luther was 15, a dissenting Dominican friar named Girolamo Savonarola had been burned at the stake for heresy.

As Luther and his companion walked south from Florence they found themselves amid crowds of pilgrims who were on their way to Rome, where they would pray, worship, and see the various "relics," or remains, of the saints and martyrs. When Luther first saw Rome in the distance, he was overcome with emotion, falling on his face and crying, "Blessed art thou, Rome, Holy Rome!" Luther's visit to Rome, however, was not to prove a source of inspiration to him. Instead, he would experience frustration, disappointment, and disillusionment.

Compared to the simple German clergy, the Italian priests were leading lives of luxury and self-indulgence. Luther described how "the Italians mocked us for being pious monks, for they hold Christians fools. They say six or seven masses in the time it takes me to say one, for they take money for it and I do not." Luther would pass relics being sold in the street—a tooth of St. Jerome's, pieces of Moses' burning bush, coins received by Judas for betraying Jesus Christ, hairs from the head of St. John, a piece of straw from Christ's cradle. The pilgrims would stop to buy relics and then continue on to shrines to pray for loved ones who had died, hoping thereby to shorten the time that their departed relatives would spend in purgatory.

At one of the most celebrated shrines Luther had a revelation of great importance. At the eastern end of the Piazza di San Giovanni was, and still is, the chapel of Sancta Sanctorum. The 28 steps of the chapel were, Catholics believed, taken from the hall in Jerusalem where Christ was condemned. Christ

*What lies there are about relics! One claims to have a feather from the wing of the angel Gabriel, and the Bishop of Mainz has a flame from Moses' burning bush. And how does it happen that 18 apostles are buried in Germany when Christ had only 12?*

—MARTIN LUTHER

had purportedly traversed them on the way to his crucifixion. Pope Leo IV had proclaimed an indulgence for every step a pilgrim climbed on his or her knees while saying special prayers. For every step, it was thought, a believer might save a family member nine years in purgatory.

Luther joined the other pilgrims on the steps, climbing on his hands and knees. Despite his objection to the low caliber of the clergymen who administered religious ceremony in Rome, he had visited many shrines, hoping to receive the benefits that were said to accrue to devout worshippers. Exhausted, Luther finally reached the top of the stairs and clambered to his feet. Suddenly, he was struck by the suspicion that what he had just done might have been utterly futile. Looking down at the other pilgrims who were huffing and puffing their way up the sacred stairs, Luther asked himself, "Who knows whether it be so?"

This was the point at which Luther began to doubt that a Christian could save a soul—his or her own, or the soul of a loved one—simply by visiting shrines and paying tithes to the Church.

About six months after his return to Erfurt from Rome, in the fall of 1511, Luther was transferred back to Wittenberg at Dr. von Staupitz's request. About a year later Luther received yet another important promotion. He was chosen, along with several other friars, to accompany von Staupitz to a meeting of senior Augustinians in the city of Cologne. Elections of priors and sub-priors were held at the conference and Luther, much to his surprise, was elected sub-prior of the Wittenberg friary.

Just a few weeks after his election, the relative tranquillity of Luther's existence was shattered by a conversation that he had with von Staupitz. The Augustinian superior suggested that it was time for Luther to take his doctorate in theology, commence preaching, and become a professor of Bible studies at the university. Though Luther was a devoted student of the Bible, he felt completely overwhelmed by von Staupitz's proposal. "You are trying to kill me," he protested. "I would not live three months." Von Staupitz merely replied, "That is quite all right. God

Florentine citizens witness the burning of religious reformer Girolamo Savonarola (1452–1498) and two other dissident monks. Luther often recalled the visit that he had made to this site in 1510, no doubt wondering if he might not suffer a similar fate himself one day.

has plenty of work for clever men to do in heaven."

Luther's somewhat hysterical response to von Staupitz's suggestion was not conditioned simply by his natural concern at the prospect of having to preach to the other friars (many of whom were much older than himself), lecture on the Bible, and pursue his own studies. While he realized that his workload would be greater than ever before, what really staggered him was the fact that, at age 28, he had been judged worthy of a qualification that even the most gifted scholars rarely gained until they were at least 40, or, more often, 50 years of age. Luther realized that, despite his relative youth and inexperience, he was being singled out by his superiors as a candidate for swift advancement.

Luther received his doctorate in theology on October 18, 1512, and immediately assumed his appointment as professor of Bible studies. The pressure under which he quickly found himself often left him physically and mentally exhausted. In 1533, reminiscing about this period of his life, Luther would write: "When I was a monk I was unwilling to omit any of the prayers, but when I was

**Crowds throng St. Peter's Square at the coronation of Pope Sixtus V (1520–1590) in 1585. In the background is the half-completed dome of the new basilica, whose construction was largely financed by the sale of indulgences.**

busy with public lecturing and writing I often accumulated my appointed prayers for a whole week, or even two or three weeks. Then I would take a Saturday off, or shut myself in for as long as three days without food or drink, until I had said the prescribed prayers. This made my head split, and as a consequence I couldn't close my eyes for five nights, lay deathly ill and went out of my senses. Soon after I had recovered and tried again to read, my head went round and round."

It was also during his early years as a professor of Bible studies that Luther began to suffer from increasingly severe bouts of depression—sensations of *Anfechtung* that were far worse than the ones that he had experienced at Erfurt.

Early in 1515 Luther received another promotion and became vicar provincial of the Augustinian Eremites. As vicar provincial Luther was responsible for the administrative and spiritual supervision of 11 Augustinian cloisters in Saxony and Thuringia.

By 1516 Luther had become one of the busiest and most highly regarded scholars in Wittenberg. In a letter written in October of that year Luther

**The front elevation for St. Peter's, as drawn by Florentine architect Antonio da Sangallo (1455–1535). Luther and his followers considered the vast amounts of money that the popes spent on this magnificent cathedral symptomatic of a materialism that had nothing to do with true faith.**

described his situation to an old friend in Erfurt: "I nearly need two copyists or secretaries. All day long I do almost nothing else than write letters. . . . I am a preacher at the monastery, I am a reader during mealtimes, I am invited daily to preach in the city church, I have to supervise the studies of the novices, I am a vicar (and that means I am eleven times prior), I am caretaker of the fishpond at Leitzkau, I represent the people of Herzberg in the court at Torgau, I lecture on Paul, and I am assembling a commentary on the Psalms. I hardly have any uninterrupted time to say the 'Hours' and celebrate Mass. Beside all this there are my own struggles with the flesh, the world, and the Devil. See what a lazy man I am!"

Luther's reference in this letter to his lectures on the writings of St. Paul gives no indication of the fact that he had reached some truly revolutionary conclusions regarding the nature of faith in the course of his researches. Indeed, the people to whom he lectured and preached had failed to recognize that the sermons he based upon his discoveries actually represented a major departure from current doctrine.

St. Paul's Letter to the Romans, upon which Luther lectured throughout 1515 and 1516, became the inspiration for his belief in faith as the way of salvation. The 17th verse of the first chapter reads: "For therein is the righteousness of God revealed from faith to faith: as it is written, The just shall live by faith." Luther's investigation of this text convinced him that Christians did not have to try harder and harder, through good deeds and self-sacrifice, to live a perfect life. Luther now began to believe that "the righteousness of God is that by which the righteous live through a gift of God, namely by faith." Luther had previously hated the phrase "righteousness of God" because he felt that such a notion portrayed God as a remote and heartless punisher of the sinful. With this revelation, however, Luther's spirits soared: "Here I felt that I was altogether born again and had entered paradise itself through open gates. There a totally other face of the entire Scripture showed itself to me. . . . So

> *He who wants to be saved should be so minded as if there were no human being but he alone, and that the consolation and promise of God through all the Scriptures concerned him only.*
>
> —MARTIN LUTHER

that place in Paul was for me truly the gate to paradise."

Luther's revelation was the turning point of his life and of the history of Christianity. The implications of the conclusions that Luther had reached are summed up as follows by Todd: "[Luther now believed that man] was always a sinner but always justified—if only he turned to Christ. It was the way of *sola fides*, faith alone, which he found through *Scriptura sola*, only through the words of Scripture, and not through [ecclesiastical] law or conventions. . . . All fear was banished in the certainty of grace. No longer was it a matter of an assent to certain doctrines, but a simple personal act of surrender, a total trust in God known in the Word, his son, Jesus [Christ]."

Many of the uncertainties that had plagued Luther for so long now simply vanished. He was at peace with himself and, as a result, would have the opportunity, for the first time in his life, to change the direction of his capacity for criticism. No longer would he needlessly persecute himself for his failings. Increasingly, Luther's thinking would turn outward, moving beyond the confines of the cloister and the university. Luther would soon find himself in confrontation with those who took a very different view of the word of God and the nature and meaning of faith.

A relief by Italian sculptor Nicola Pisano (1220–1284) portrays sinners suffering the torments of hell. It was on ordinary believers' fears of such punishment that the sellers of indulgences preyed for hundreds of years until Luther's teachings encouraged people to abandon their superstitions.

1520

# 5

# The Contender

> *I will give myself as a Christ to my neighbor just as Christ offered himself to me.*
> —MARTIN LUTHER

By 1516 Luther was one of the most popular and respected professors at the University of Wittenberg. He preached to his brethren in the Augustinian cloister and also delivered sermons in the Wittenberg Castle church. The townspeople loved to hear him speak. The earthiness and occasional brutality of the language that he employed often shocked his audiences. He spoke his mind in a manner that was both clear and direct. At first his insights into faith did not provoke him to question the supremacy of the Church in spiritual matters or to disparage its practices. He only wanted to change academic theology by reawakening Christians to the Bible's teachings on faith, on justification by faith, and on grace—the merciful favor that God shows to man even when man has not deserved it.

Luther's routine of teaching and preaching was to change, however, following the arrival of an indulgence seller in the nearby town of Jüterborg. The abuses that Luther had seen in Rome were soon to be visited upon his homeland.

At this time, Pope Leo X needed money to finance the construction of St. Peter's Cathedral in Rome. Consequently, when Prince Albrecht of Brandenburg came to him offering to make a deal, the pope

**Prince Albrecht of Brandenburg (1490–1545), as portrayed by Albrecht Dürer (1471–1528). In 1514, to secure his appointment as archbishop of Mainz, Albrecht paid Pope Leo X a large sum of money and authorized the sale of indulgences throughout his domains. Half of the profits from the indulgences went toward the construction of St. Peter's.**

**Luther as a doctor of theology c. 1516, by which time he had become one of the most popular and respected professors at the University of Wittenberg. During this period, Luther's researches into St. Paul's Letter to the Romans led him to conclusions regarding the nature of faith that ran counter to Catholic doctrine.**

was willing to listen. The 24-year-old Albrecht, who was also archbishop of Magdeburg and administrator of the diocese of Halberstadt, was eager to acquire a third ecclesiastical appointment—the archbishopric of Mainz. It soon became apparent that even though Albrecht was, due to his youth, technically ineligible for such a major ecclesiastical office, he would have no trouble striking a bargain with the pope. Leo, as a member of the immensely wealthy de Medici dynasty, tended to regard the papacy as little more than an extension of his family's business empire. It was quickly agreed that Albrecht, in exchange for papal approval of his request, would pay a large sum of money to the pope and then collect indulgences throughout the principality of Brandenburg. Half of the profits would go toward the building of St. Peter's, the other half to the Fugger banking house, which had contracted to loan Albrecht the money that he was to pay to the pope. Leo then declared that the indulgence would become effective on March 31, 1515, and last for eight years.

In deciding to add yet another indulgence to the many that were already being dispensed in Germany, Leo was continuing his established policy of capitalizing on the fact that Germany, as a component territory of an empire that had been in decline for centuries, did not have a powerful ruler of its own to defend its interests. Germany had known no equivalent of national leaders like the kings of England and France, who had, on many occasions, successfully rejected papal nominees to religious appointments and had also defied the decisions handed down by the Church's courts. Leo had made it quite clear, from the outset of his reign, that he considered Germany particularly ripe for exploitation by indulgence sellers.

Johann Tetzel, a Dominican friar, represented Albrecht in selling the indulgences. He traveled the length and breadth of Brandenburg, delivering his sermons on the efficacy of indulgences and persuading people to purchase his guarantees of divine pardon. When Luther learned the details of Tetzel's visit to Jüterborg, he became incensed.

According to Luther's parishioners, Tetzel entered the town behind an official carrying a cross decorated with the papal insignia and at the head of a procession of Jüterborg's leading citizens. Another official held aloft a gold cushion on which was placed the pope's proclamation of indulgence—the document authorizing dispensation of indulgences.

Once the cross had been set up in the market place, Tetzel began to speak: "Visit the most holy cross erected before you and ever imploring you. . . . Consider that all who are contrite and have confessed and made contribution will receive complete remission of all their sins. Listen to the voices of your dear dead relatives and friends . . . saying 'Pity us, pity us. We are in dire torment from which you can redeem us for a pittance.' Remember that you are able to redeem them, for

> As soon as the coin in the coffer rings
> The soul from purgatory springs

Will you not then for a few pennies receive these letters of indulgence through which you are able to lead a divine and immortal soul into the fatherland of paradise?"

Luther found Tetzel's activities and the fact that they were sanctioned and encouraged by the papacy an affront to Christianity. For Luther, faith was the only way of salvation. He firmly believed that the pope had no right to lay claim to jurisdiction over purgatory.

Many ordinary Germans found themselves in sympathy with Luther's expressions of outrage. Though Germany was divided into many separate states, the German people were beginning to develop a strong sense of national pride. They resented the way in which much of Germany's money was being spent on the beautification of Rome.

According to a legend now known to have no basis in fact, Luther made his stand on October 31, 1517. He took a hammer and some nails and posted a text containing 95 theses, or propositions for debate, on the door of the Wittenberg Castle church. Though he had not intended the theses for publication, they were widely reprinted throughout Germany. The

ALINARI/ART RESOURCE

**Pope Leo X (1475–1521), as portrayed by Raffaello Sanzio (1483–1520), who is more commonly known as Raphael. Leo X, a member of the powerful de Medici family, occupied the papal throne at the outset of Luther's revolt against the Church. His reign epitomized the luxury and grandeur of the Renaissance papacy.**

A self-portrait by the famous German painter and engraver Albrecht Dürer. When the Church authorities began to step up their campaign of condemnation against Luther, Dürer sent the beleaguered theologian a woodcut as a token of his admiration and support.

German people finally had a voice speaking out on their behalf against the questionable practices to which the Church was willing to resort in its quest for wealth.

Luther's theses were forceful and direct: 21) Those preachers of Indulgences are wrong when they say that a man is absolved and saved from every penalty by the Pope's Indulgences. . . . 23) If any remission of all penalties whatsoever can be granted to anyone, it can only be to those who are most perfect, in other words to very few. . . . 51) Christians should be taught that, if the Pope knew the exactions of the preachers of Indulgences, he would rather have the basilica of St. Peter reduced to ashes rather than built with the skin, flesh, and bones of his sheep.

Having posted his argument for inspection by the people of Wittenberg, Luther then sent a copy of the text to Prince Albrecht, along with a letter accusing him of having "a fearful and growing reckoning to pay." But Albrecht was only one of the many people who were to receive copies of Luther's arguments. The famous painter and engraver Albrecht Dürer, who had once worked in Wittenberg, sent Luther a woodcut as a mark of his gratitude. And, of course, the pope himself received a copy of Luther's theses, which had been forwarded to him by Prince Albrecht.

At first, Pope Leo X believed that Luther must have been drunk when he wrote the theses and that he would quickly repent once sober. He began to take Luther at his word, however, when the Church's earnings from indulgences dispensed in Germany showed signs of diminution. Many of Luther's friends were disturbed by the pope's anger and became afraid that their dissident colleague might one day burn at the stake.

Many Roman Catholics had criticized the sale of indulgences since the practice was first established in the 12th century. However, the wider implications of Luther's attack on the selling of indulgences meant that his position might come to be declared heretical. Luther recognized that any popular support shown to a would-be reformer might erode very quickly should that person be accused of heresy. He could remember having seen the square in Florence where Savonarola had been executed in 1498 for ignoring a papal order instructing him to desist from his criticism of the Church. (Savonarola had been virtual ruler of Florence following the popular overthrow of the city's ruling dynasty in 1494, but his defiance of Pope Alexander VI proved to be his downfall.) And now Luther was similarly committed to standing by his principles and felt unable to retract a single statement, even if it meant risking death.

Pope Leo became increasingly determined to put a stop to Luther's activities. His first move was to call upon Giles Viterbo, the superior general of the Augustinians, "to quiet that man, for newly kindled flames are easily quenched." When it became apparent that Viterbo felt little obligation to respond, the pope turned to the Dominicans and to Sylvester Prierias, a senior churchman in Rome. Prierias devised an exceptionally violent refutation of the theses, and referred to Luther as "a leper with a brain of brass and a nose of iron." As a prominent

*Any truly repentant Christian has a right to full remission of penalty and guilt, even without indulgence letters.*
—MARTIN LUTHER
quoted from the 95 Theses

The exquisite interior of the dome of St. Peter's. In the explications to his 95 Theses, or propositions for debate, which he wrote in 1517, Luther lashed out at the Church's rapacious taxation of Europe's Christians to finance the construction of St. Peter's, declaring: "The revenues of all Christendom are being sucked into this insatiable basilica."

member of the Catholic hierarchy, Prierias argued that the pope was infallible—that "his judgment is the oracle of God." Prierias's attack on the dissident Wittenberger's theses came in the wake of a similar written assault that had been devised by Tetzel himself toward the end of 1517. But neither Prierias's nor Tetzel's arguments could sway Luther or his followers. In fact, when a messenger arrived in Wittenberg with 800 copies of Tetzel's pamphlet, the university students waylaid him and burned them.

As he preached and wrote in defense of his position, Luther became increasingly aware of the possibility that his chosen path might lead him to trial and execution. Suddenly, he was emerging as the leader of a religious revolt. Despite the inner tranquillity that he had come to know following what he considered to be his rediscovery of the true meaning of St. Paul's writings on the nature of faith, Luther realized that the growing controversy surrounding his teachings might eventually develop into a conflict that would disturb both his own peace of mind and that of many other Christians.

**A contemporary engraving shows Luther posting his 95 Theses in 1517. One of the most radical elements of the comprehensive attack on the Church represented by Luther's theses was his questioning of the doctrine of papal infallibility.**

# 6

# The Disputant

Luther was overwhelmed by the German people's enthusiastic response to his theses. The controversy aroused by the theses was even exploited by Germany's princes, who used it as a political tool in their feuding with each other. One prince in particular, Frederick III, elector of Saxony, became deeply involved in this dispute that had been started by a young friar from the Saxon town of Wittenberg. Frederick was one of the candidates in the upcoming election for a new Holy Roman emperor.

At that time, Emperor Maximilian, who was in poor health and not expected to live much longer, was desperate to ensure that his grandson, Charles Habsburg, would be elected to succeed him. Accordingly, he began to attempt to buy the electors' votes. The pope was horrified. The election of Charles, who already ruled the Netherlands, the French-speaking province Burgundy, and most of Spain, would put one man in control of half of Europe and pose a serious threat to the political power of the Church and the influential Italian families associated with it. In his desperation to secure the election of a candidate who would pose little or no threat to the interests of the Church, Leo began

THE METROPOLITAN MUSEUM OF ART, GIFT OF ROBERT LEHMAN, 1946.

**Elector Frederick III of Saxony (1486–1525) was Luther's most powerful ally during the early stages of the Reformation. Frederick's decision to support Luther had as much to do with politics as with religion, since he recognized the appeal that Luther's teachings held for Germany's nationalists.**

Bohemian religious reformer John Huss (1369–1415) is burned at the stake following his condemnation as a heretic. In 1519 Luther's defense of several of the positions taken by Huss and his followers was largely instrumental in Pope Leo X's decision to denounce him officially.

doing his best to outbid Maximilian and to gain Frederick's support.

In August 1518 the authorities in Rome began to exert diplomatic pressure on the leaders of the Church in Germany. They denounced Luther and requested that he come to Rome to defend his position. Hearing of this development, Maximilian, who was presiding at a *Diet*, or imperial conference, in Augsburg, wrote to Rome and demanded that strong measures be taken against Luther. Leo and his colleagues were overjoyed at the emperor's reaction to the situation and immediately referred the matter to the papal representative to the Diet, Cardinal Thomas de Vio, who was also known as Cajetan. The papal legate was ordered to secure Luther's arrest and to obtain letters of assistance from the emperor and Elector Frederick.

About two weeks later, however, it became apparent that the pope had reminded himself that the Church stood to gain more from Frederick's election than it did from the arrest of one of the elector's favorite professors. Frederick was known to be proud of his new university in Wittenberg and more than a little sympathetic toward the most controversial man on its staff. The pope, though surprised by Frederick's reluctance to comply with Cajetan's request, agreed to let Luther remain in Germany. Leo had made the mistake of failing to take account of the burgeoning nationalism of the German people.

It was then arranged that Luther and Cajetan would meet at Augsburg. Cajetan was under strict orders to ensure that the meeting did not turn into an academic debate. Luther was simply to recant in Cajetan's presence. Leo had made it clear that he would be willing to forget the entire affair if Luther would simply stop questioning papal authority and Catholic doctrine.

Upon his arrival in Augsburg, Luther went to the house of the Carmelite Friars, whose superior was also a graduate of Wittenberg. Lawyers appointed by the elector advised Luther not to set foot in the streets until he received a letter from Maximilian's office guaranteeing his safe conduct. Having re-

*Martin is of medium height with a gaunt body that has been so exhausted by studies and worries that one can almost count the bones under his skin. Yet one can see in him that God's strength is with him in his difficult undertaking.*

—PETER MOSELLANUS
rector of the University of
Wittenberg, writing in 1520

ceived this vital documentation, Luther, accompanied by von Staupitz and the lawyers, proceeded to the Fugger mansion, where Cajetan and his retinue had taken up residence.

Cajetan, one of the foremost theologians of the Catholic church, was known to be an ultra-papalist who regarded the papacy as a divine institution. Both parties to the dispute recognized that the confrontation would be extremely difficult and fraught with dangerous consequences. The first meeting took place on October 12, 1518; two more followed within a few days. Having been instructed either to make Luther admit his errors and submit to papal authority or to arrest him and escort him back to Rome if he proved intractable, Cajetan kept discussion to a minimum.

At the end of the third meeting Cajetan, whom Luther considered "no more able to handle this discussion than is an ass to play a harp," lost his temper and ordered Luther to leave and not return until he was prepared to recant. Cajetan also made it clear that he would not be exceeding his authority as papal legate should he choose to throw Luther and von Staupitz into prison. When Cajetan then failed to reply to Luther's request for another hearing, von Staupitz decided that Luther should be released from his vows. Von Staupitz realized that Luther might be forced to flee for his life at any moment, and that precious time might easily be lost if he remained under any obligation to confer with his superiors before making a move. Shortly after von Staupitz had released him from his vows, Luther, aided by his friends, escaped from Augsburg under cover of darkness.

Following his return to Wittenberg, Luther wrote a report of his interviews with Cajetan. Part of his account reads thus: "I see that books are published and various rumors scattered abroad about what I did at Augsburg, although truly I did nothing there but lose the time and expense of the journey . . . for I was instructed there that to teach the truth is the same as to disturb the Church, but to flatter men and deny Christ is considered the same as pacifying and exalting the Church of Christ."

*A spinner or a seamstress teaches her daughter her trade while she is young, but now even the most learned bishops and prelates do not know the Gospel.*
—MARTIN LUTHER

Cajetan's lack of success persuaded the pope to revise his approach to the Luther case. He decided that, having failed to profit from intimidation and coercion, he would increase his efforts to win the allegiance of Elector Frederick. Leo sent flattering letters to the elector and his nobles, and awarded Frederick the prestigious Golden Rose. (Leo's award of the Golden Rose to Frederick can almost be considered a bribe, since this honor was generally conferred upon Catholic princes who had shown outstanding loyalty to the Church.) Leo also sent another representative, Karl von Miltitz, instructing him to arrest Luther if he refused to recant. However, circumstances were soon to oblige von Miltitz not to press Luther as violently as had Cajetan.

Following the death of Emperor Maximilian on January 12, 1519, Leo became increasingly concerned about securing the election of a successor who would serve the Church's purpose. There were three candidates for the position: Charles Habsburg; King Francis I of France; and Frederick. Leo, maintaining his support for Frederick and adhering to his policy of not doing anything to alienate the elector, instructed von Miltitz to adopt a more conciliatory attitude toward Luther until after the election, which was scheduled to take place in June. Von Miltitz did, however, make it clear to Frederick that in the pope's estimation Luther's teachings were the greatest threat the Church had faced in more than 1,000 years. He also informed the elector that his cooperation in the matter would be richly rewarded. When von Miltitz suggested that Frederick might even be allowed to appoint a cardinal, the elector became convinced that he was being informed, albeit indirectly, that his nomination of a compliant Luther might well receive papal approval. The deviousness that von Miltitz displayed in his overtures to Frederick was also due, to some extent, to his awareness of the political situation inside Germany. He realized that there was little to be gained by alienating Luther's protector in a land where, as he had discovered for himself in countless conversations with peasants and townspeople, most people were solidly behind Luther.

In February 1519 Luther began to prepare for a debate that was to be held in Leipzig in July. Four months later, on June 28, Charles Habsburg was elected Holy Roman emperor. However, the fact of Charles's election did not mean that Leo was now free to initiate an uncompromising diplomatic assault against Elector Frederick. Since the emperor was much preoccupied with the affairs of Spain, Frederick was to remain the most important figure in German politics for a while longer. The pope therefore decided that summary action would be inadvisable.

In July 1519 Luther mounted a wagon and began the 40-mile journey from Wittenberg to Leipzig. Seated beside him was his good friend Philip Melanchthon, professor of Greek at the University of Wittenberg. Behind the cart walked almost 200 students carrying battle-axes and sticks. Awaiting them in Leipzig was Luther's debating opponent, a Bavarian named Johann Eck, professor at the Uni-

**Luther defends his teachings before the pope's representative, Cardinal Thomas de Vio (1469–1534), at Augsburg in 1518. De Vio, whom the angry Luther described as "no more able to handle this discussion than is an ass to play a harp," was an ultrapapalist who sincerely believed the papacy to be a divine institution.**

**Dr. Johann Eck (1486– 1543), whom Luther debated at Leipzig in 1519. A talented disputant and respected theologian, Eck manipulated the debate with incredible skill, forcing Luther to reveal the full implications of his teachings, and demonstrating that his opponent's ideas constituted a radical departure from accepted Catholic belief.**

versity of Ingolstadt and one of the most learned theologians of his day.

Eck had become involved in the controversy surrounding Luther's theses early in 1518, when he wrote one of the first and most comprehensive refutations of Luther's position. Luther knew that the impending debate, though intended as a purely academic affair, might turn out to be the most important he had ever attended in the context of his confrontation with the Church. Luther knew that Eck would subject his teachings to the most sustained and searching criticism that they had yet received. He had prepared pages and pages of notes on the finer points of Church history and Canon Law—the great legal code of Christendom. Dr. Eck, who had been the first to accuse him of radically departing from Catholic orthodoxy, was widely acknowledged to be an exceptionally talented disputant and was undoubtedly the most dangerous opponent that Luther had ever been called upon to face.

As the army from Wittenberg approached Leipzig, they saw the flags of George, duke of Albertine Saxony, flying from the steeples of the town's many churches. The students prepared their axes. In the distance, they could see teeming crowds of knights, students, and townspeople. Anticipating a possible outburst of violence between the Wittenbergers and Eck's supporters, the Leipzig town council had provided Eck with a 76-man bodyguard.

Luther and Eck debated for 18 days. One of those present described the two contestants thus: "Martin is of middle height, emaciated from care and study, so that you can almost count his bones through his skin. He is in the vigour of manhood and has a clear, penetrating voice. He is learned and has the Scripture at his fingers' ends. . . . A perfect forest of words and ideas stands at his command. . . . He is equal to anything. In company he is vivacious, jocose, always cheerful and gay no matter how hard his adversaries press him. Eck is a heavy, square-set fellow with a full German voice supported by a hefty chest. He would make a tragedian or town crier, but his voice is rather rough than clear. His eyes and mouth and his whole face remind one more of a butcher than a theologian."

The discussions often grew heated. Eck and Luther began by debating the primacy of the pope and the inviolability of rulings made by Church councils. The debate then focused on such interrelated questions as purgatory, indulgences, and the power of a priest to forgive sins. Dr. Eck very cleverly drew comparisons between Luther's beliefs and those espoused by John Huss, a Bohemian heretic who had been burned at the stake in 1415. When pressed to comment on Huss, whose greatest crime had been to suggest that both popes and Church councils could sometimes be mistaken, Luther said clearly and forcefully, "It is certain that among the articles of John Huss and the Bohemians there are many which are most Christian . . . which the universal Church is not able to condemn." At this point, according to Luther, "the adder swelled up, exaggerated my crime, and nearly went insane in his adulation of the Leipzig audience." This was the moment for which Luther's opponent had been waiting; Luther had defended a heretic. It made no difference to a papalist like Eck that Luther had

A 16th-century engraving shows Luther preaching against the abuses of the Church. The avaricious agents of the papacy are being consumed by a flaming beast from hell, while the common people are portrayed as allies of the crucified Christ.

discovered that one of the statements made by Huss and condemned by the Council of Constance in 1415 was derived directly from St. Augustine and should, therefore, have been perfectly acceptable to the Church.

The audience became agitated; Duke George, recalling the stories of how Huss's followers had invaded Saxony, leaving a trail of death and destruction in their wake, shook his head and shouted: "The plague!"

Having been drawn onto such incredibly dangerous ground by Eck's successful manipulation of the debate, Luther began to realize that there were more issues at stake than the legitimacy of indulgences. His position was much more perilous now that he had openly challenged the authority of the pope and the supreme councils of the Church; he had defended a heretic; he had refused to heed the warnings of the pope's representatives. He had never

intended to cause divisions within the Christian faith or to reject the teachings of the Catholic church. It was now apparent, however, that in his determination to preach the priority of faith he might prove to have signed his own death warrant.

Luther departed from Leipzig feeling exhausted and defeated. As he described it, "The citizens of Leipzig never greeted us nor visited us, but acted like the bitterest enemies; but Eck they followed and clung to and invited to dinners in their houses and gave him a robe and a chamois-hair gown. They escorted him around on horseback; in fact they tried everything they could think of to insult me."

Luther was soon to discover that the enemies he had made in Leipzig were few in comparison with those he would encounter beyond its walls. He had only just begun to proclaim the revolutionary message of faith that would change the face of Christianity forever.

**Still to be seen above the high altar of the Wittenberg Castle church, this painting by Cranach shows Luther delivering a sermon to the townspeople. The apparition of Christ at center symbolizes Luther's vision of Christ as mediator between man and God.**

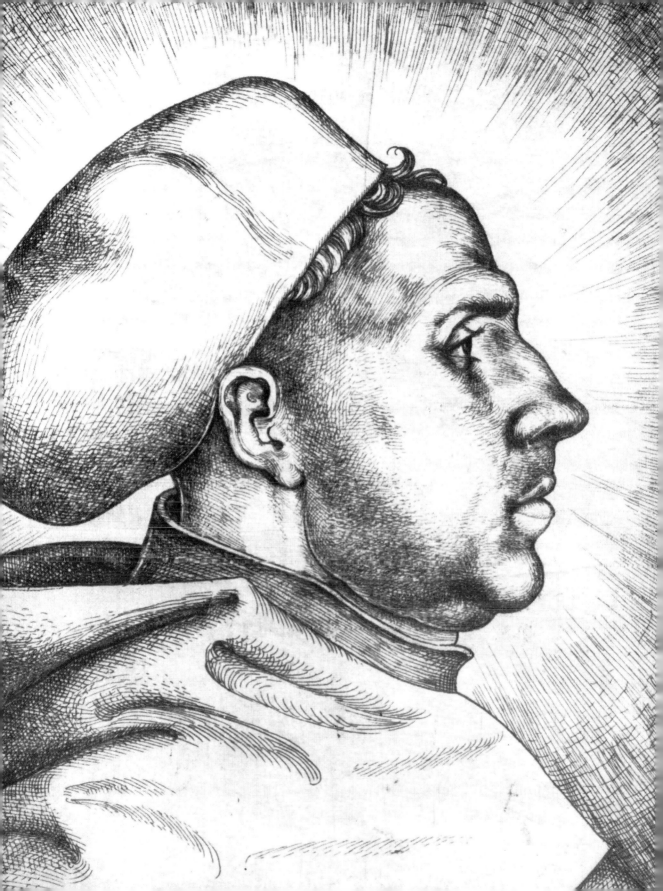

# 7

# The Challenger

Upon their return to Wittenberg, the despondent Luther and his downcast followers resumed their duties at the university and at the cloister. Luther's mood was not improved by reports that Dr. Eck had left Leipzig and was now denouncing his teachings to scholars at the universities of Cologne and Louvain, both of which institutions were renowned for extreme conservatism in matters of religion. Luther's bitterness at the hostility that the people of Leipzig had shown toward him emerges very clearly from a letter that he wrote to his friend Georg Spalatin just a few days after his return: "Whereas we had hoped for harmony between the people of Wittenberg and Leipzig, they acted so aggressively that I fear it will seem that discord and enmity were actually born here. This is the fruit of human glory. I, who really restrain my impetuosity cannot but vomit out my dislike of them, for I am flesh and blood, and their hatred was very shameless and their injustice was quite shameless—it was thoroughly wrong to be so lacking in fair play in so sacred a matter."

Luther's disgust at the manner in which his opponents in Leipzig had reduced theology to little more than a political and intellectual punching bag inspired him to make his position even clearer. By

The title page of *To the Christian Nobility of the German Nation Concerning the Reform of the Christian Estate*, which Luther wrote in 1520. At the very end of this pivotal treatise Luther wrote: "May God grant us all a Christian understanding, and especially to the Christian nobility of the German nation true spiritual courage, to do what is best for our unhappy Church."

Luther as he appeared in 1520, by which time he had completed three revolutionary treatises that are now considered to have been the cornerstone of the Reformation: *To the Christian Nobility of the German Nation Concerning the Reform of the Christian Estate*, *Prelude on the Babylonian Captivity of the Church*, and *The Freedom of a Christian Man*.

75

An engraving by Cranach points out the parallels between two famous dissenters—Luther and Huss. The similarities between his own cause and Huss's were not lost upon Luther, who once wrote: "They will cook a goose [*Huss* is German for goose] now but after 100 years they will hear a swan sing. . . ."

the middle of 1520 he was close to completing three of his most important and influential treatises.

The first of these, written in German and entitled *To the Christian Nobility of the German Nation Concerning the Reform of the Christian Estate*, called upon the Holy Roman emperor and the German ruling class to initiate a major reform of the Church. Since Church and state were so intertwined at that time, Luther's exhortation essentially constituted a demand for the reform of society. He was appealing to the secular authorities to free Germany from papal domination. He encouraged the Germans to abandon their dependency on Roman laws and rituals. He also criticized many traditional Catholic rituals, the pride and selfishness of the Catholic clergy, and the doctrine that held that the pope's interpretation of the Bible was both correct and not to be disputed. Luther made a particularly concerted assault on the fact that, under Church law, priests enjoyed preferment over ordinary believers: "We are all alike Christians and have baptism, faith, the [Holy] Spirit, and all things alike. If a priest is killed, a land is laid under an interdict. Why not in the case of a peasant? Whence comes this great distinction between those who are called Christians?"

Another important element of this treatise was Luther's denunciation of the institution of priestly celibacy. He had come to believe that priests should be allowed to marry, and his comments on the subject were particularly scathing. He declared that, when a Catholic priest required the services of a housekeeper, any attempt by the Church to enforce that priest's celibacy was "like putting straw and fire together and forbidding them to burn. . . . The pope has as little power to command this as he has to forbid eating, drinking . . . or growing fat."

The second treatise, written in Latin and entitled *Prelude on the Babylonian Captivity of the Church* was addressed to scholars, theologians, and the clergy. In this tract, which Todd describes as an attack on the "veritable deportation of the Christian people to the papal tyranny," Luther criticized many of the rituals of the Mass and the entire system of sacraments—the various rites and practices of the Church. So powerful and uncompromising was this treatise that, upon reading it, the renowned Dutch humanist Erasmus declared: "The breach is irreparable." Bainton explains Erasmus's reaction thus: "The reason was that the pretensions of the Roman Catholic church rest so completely upon the sacraments as the exclusive channels of grace and upon the prerogatives of the clergy, by whom the sacraments are exclusively administered. If sacramentalism is undercut, then [dependency on the priesthood] is bound to fall."

There were seven sacraments: marriage; ordination; extreme unction; confirmation; penance; the Mass; and baptism. Luther, believing that the only true sacraments were those that constituted external signs of a solely Christian *and* Christ-instituted grace, acknowledged only two—baptism and the Mass. Since marriage was also practiced by the Jews and the Muslims, Luther failed to see why the institution should be accorded any kind of exclusivity within Christianity. Because the ordination of priests was a rite of the Church and had not been instituted by Christ, Luther could not acknowledge its validity. Extreme unction (the Catholic practice of anointing a dying person with oil) seemed to Luther mere superstition. He considered the Catholic practice of confirming a believer in the faith invalid for the same reason that he rejected ordination. Luther believed that penance—making amends for one's sins—could be viewed as a minor sacrament, mainly because Christ had once said to his followers "Be penitent." Confessing one's sins he thought useful, but not to be institutionalized. Luther firmly believed that sacraments other than baptism and the Mass were false inasmuch as they had been prescribed by the papacy, an institution that he considered human and historical rather than divine.

One of the most controversial elements of this treatise was Luther's rejection of transubstantiation, the miracle that, according to Catholic doctrine, occurs when the priest administers the sacred bread and wine during the Mass. For Luther, the bread and wine dispensed to communicants by the

> *Baptism is water with the Word of God, and this is the essence and whole susbstance of baptism. When, therefore, water and God's Word are conjoined, it must necessarily be holy and divine water, for as the Word is, so the water becomes also.*
>
> —MARTIN LUTHER

priest were not, as Catholics still believe, the actual flesh and blood of Christ. Luther denied that any such miracle could be performed by the word of man. However, because the precedent for the Mass was Christ's "Last Supper," the meal that Christ took with his disciples before he died and at which he declared the bread and wine to be his body and blood, Luther believed the Mass to be of paramount sacramental value. According to Bainton, Luther believed God to be "a hidden God who has chosen to make himself known at three points: in the flesh of Christ, in the word embedded in Scripture, and in the elements of the sacrament." Because of this, Luther was convinced that the priest, in administering the Mass, does not *make* God. Luther viewed the Mass as a ritual of communion with God and Jesus Christ, and, equally important, as a rite of fellowship with other believers.

Related to Luther's assault on several of the sacraments was his declaration that all believers were priests. He wrote: "Not only are we most free kings of all, but we are priests forever, by which priesthood we can appear before God, pray for one another and teach one another." Luther was arguing that Christians both could and should be responsible for their own spiritual well-being: "All Christians possess a truly spiritual status and among them there is no distinction save that of function. This is so because we possess one baptism, one faith, one gospel, and are equal as Christians. Anyone who has emerged from the waters of baptism may pride himself on already being ordained priest, bishop or pope, although not everyone may be suited to exercise such an office. Therefore let every congregation elect a devout citizen to be their priest."

Whereas in the other two treatises Luther dealt with the outward displays of religion—the practices of the clergy, the role of the pope, and the sacramental system—in the third treatise he set forth the essence of his understanding of the Christian life. Entitled *The Freedom of a Christian Man*, the work began with a seemingly paradoxical assertion, taken from St. Paul's writings in the New Testament, regarding the nature of Christian freedom:

**Dutch scholar and theologian Desiderius Erasmus (1466–1536), as painted by German artist Hans Holbein (1465–1524). The full implications of Luther's attack on the various rites and practices of the Church in *Prelude on the Babylonian Captivity of the Church* were immediately apparent to Erasmus, who, upon reading the tract, declared: "The breach is irreparable."**

"A Christian is a free lord of all, subject to none. A Christian is a dutiful servant, subject to all."

More clearly stated, the Christian act, by definition, is an act of compassion and brotherly love. Such an act is never simply a mere following of rules or adherence to a body of laws, but is rather an expression of deep faith in God. According to Luther, the Christian is most free because he or she acts from the heart and does so without regard for the dictates of others. Consequently, the Christian is also obliged to act out of unqualified and unconditional love.

The three treatises were published in August, October, and November of 1520, respectively, just 15

years after Luther had vowed to St. Anne that he would become a monk. Though he had entered the cloister wanting to believe in every aspect of Catholic teachings and intending to follow every rule that governed life within his chosen order, he had now come to deny almost all the religious practices that at one time had given his life meaning and direction. The three treatises expanded upon the central belief that Luther had carried with him since his revelation concerning what he believed to be the true meaning of the verse in Romans that read, "The just shall live by faith."

Even as Germany's printers began to make unprecedented profits from the sale of Luther's books

A 16th-century woodcut portrays Luther and Elector Frederick witnessing the baptism of Christ. Although Luther disliked works of art that sought to glorify him, such portrayals of the famous dissident as one who enjoyed a special relationship with God became common even before his death.

**Bulla contra Erro res Martini Lutheri et sequarium.**

The title page of the official papal Bull, or proclamation, of excommunication issued against Luther by Leo X in 1520. The document condemned 41 of Luther's propositions, forbade him to preach, and ordered that his books be burned. The inscription above the papal insignia reads: "A proclamation against the errors of Martin Luther and his followers."

and pamphlets, the repercussions of the Leipzig debate were beginning to make themselves felt in Wittenberg. Dr. Eck had not only persuaded the pope to issue an outright condemnation of Luther but had also personally devised much of the text for this critically important communication. Leo himself composed a preface and a conclusion for the document. It was from the first two words of the preface that the *Bull*, or papal proclamation, received its official title—*Exsurge Domine* ("Arise, O Lord . . ."). The fact that Leo was enjoying a few days at his hunting lodge when Eck sought his approval for the bulk of the text probably explains why, in the second sentence of the preface, the pope described Luther as a wild boar that had invaded God's vineyard.

Against the advice of two of his cardinals, who considered the text both inaccurate and unscholarly, Leo had signed the Bull on June 16, 1520. The document condemned 41 of Luther's propositions, forbade him to preach, ordered that all his books be burned, and demanded that he either recant or face excommunication—expulsion from the Church. He was to be allowed 60 days from the time of receipt in which to arrive at a decision.

Luther received the Bull on October 11, 1520. He was astounded by what he considered its marked lack of intellectual and spiritual integrity. He wrote: "The sheer extent of the Blasphemies in the Bull overwhelms me . . . I am convinced that the last day is almost here. The reign of anti-Christ is beginning."

Shortly after receiving the Bull, Luther wrote a polemic in defense of his position. This tract, which Luther entitled *Against the Accursed Bull of Anti-Christ*, did little to improve his standing with the Catholic hierarchy. Luther referred to Rome as a city "which devours its inhabitants, never having kept faith nor keeping it now, where the most sacred fathers kill their beloved sons for the love of God, and brothers destroy brothers in obedience to Christ, as is the Roman custom and style."

By November 1520 reports had reached Wittenberg that Luther's books were being burned in Cologne, in Louvain, and in other cities.

At 9:00 A.M. on December 10, 1520, the day upon which the papal deadline for Luther's recantation expired, a crowd gathered at the Elster Gate in Wittenberg. Luther had piled up wood next to a heap of papers, books, and letters. He knelt down and struck a flint. The wood caught fire and smoke began to encircle the onlookers. In an audacious act, Luther publicly burned the Bull *Exsurge Domine*.

The shivering crowd watched in silence as the pages of the pope's letter curled amid the crackling timbers, blackened and were quickly consumed. Students brought books of Canon Law and effigies of the pope to contribute to the blaze. Some professors threw in copies of their own Catholic theology books and the writings of Dr. Eck. Luther, perfectly aware of the possible consequences of his protest, said nothing at first. Then, turning to the crowd, he gave a short speech. The words that he addressed to the assembled Wittenbergers were essentially intended for the ears of the pope: "Because thou hast brought down the truth of God, he also brings thee to this fire today. Amen."

Luther would continue to write, ever challenging the Church and appealing to the German people. But the Bull *Exsurge Domine*, though reduced to ashes at the Elster Gate, would remain a document with which to be reckoned.

**With the students and towns-people of Wittenberg looking on, Luther burns the Bull *Exsurge Domine* on December 10, 1520. *Exsurge Domine* was the Bull in which Leo X had threatened to excommunicate Luther unless he agreed to recant; its destruction resulted in Luther's excommunication three months later.**

# 8

# The Outcast

Since Luther had failed to recant by the appointed date, he was now an excommunicant. His situation was rendered even more perilous by the fact that Charles Habsburg, who was now Emperor Charles V, had begun to take a keen personal interest in the controversy. The new ruler, while realizing that the Luther case would have to be brought to a conclusion, found it difficult to arrive at a decision. Neither Charles nor the electors wished to alienate the vast majority of their people by cracking down on the man who had by now become a focus for German nationalism.

As an excommunicant, Luther was now protected only by the civil authorities. He realized that such protection would be withdrawn immediately should the emperor too decide to condemn him.

The task of securing an imperial condemnation of Luther was taken up with particular alacrity by a papal ambassador named Hieronymus Aleander. In his eagerness to have Luther sent to Rome to stand trial and face possible execution, Aleander had been putting pressure on Frederick, who was now the senior elector. Frederick, however, still favored Luther, as did the emperor, albeit less wholeheartedly. Even when, in January 1521, he received

Luther during the early stages of the Reformation, as painted by Cranach. In April 1521 the excommunicated Luther found himself deprived of the protection of the civil authorities when Charles V declared that he was "determined to proceed against him as a notorious heretic."

A woodcut entitled *The Troubled Church in a Sea of Discontent* creates a powerful impression of the effect that Luther's dissent had upon the Church, destroying the monolithic unity that had characterized the first 1,500 years of its existence.

the Bull *Decet Romanum*, which confirmed Luther's excommunication, Frederick maintained his delaying tactics. Because the Bull accused him of having encouraged Luther's heresy, Frederick declared the document inaccurate and sent it back to Rome for revision. Finally, in February 1521, Charles came to a compromise decision. Having been informed by the electors in no uncertain terms that they disliked Rome's demands, the emperor conceded to his subordinates and agreed to give Luther a hearing in Germany. Charles ordered Luther to attend the Diet that was then in session in the city of Worms. There, Luther would have the opportunity to give a full account of his beliefs.

Luther's impending defense of his position had now become the most pressing issue confronting the imperial government. It would be critically important, both to Luther's future and to the political stability of Germany. Since it seemed that the majority of the German people supported Luther, the emperor could not condemn him without running the risk of triggering a popular insurrection. However, despite the precariousness of the situation, Charles proceeded to reassert his slightly dented authority by issuing an imperial edict banning Luther's writings. Aleander, who had been greatly dismayed by the emperor's decision to summon Luther to Worms rather than have him handed over to the Church, was ecstatic.

"Expect anything of me except flight or recantation," Luther wrote to a friend before departing for Worms. "I will not flee, much less recant!" Armed with a letter of safe conduct from the emperor, Luther set out on April 2. His determination to put his case uncompromisingly and without fear grew increasingly strong during the journey. All along the route, hundreds of Germans cheered him on his way, welcoming him to their towns and calling upon God to protect him. Luther's spirits soared.

Thousands of people witnessed Luther's arrival in Worms on April 16, 1521. Aleander, continuing his efforts to cast Luther in the role of an enemy of God and the Church, was more than willing to believe reports that some priests had attempted to kiss the

Uon dem grossen
Lutherischen Narren wie in
doctor Murner beschworen hat, etc.

202. Titelblatt einer satirischen Flugschrift wider Luther

**This pamphlet entitled "As in the Great Lutheran Fool" was one of the thousands of similar tracts penned by Luther's opponents in the opening stages of the Reformation.**

hem of Luther's habit. He also said that Luther, before entering his lodgings, had stared at the crowd "with his demonic eyes."

The verbal battle between Luther and von Eck, an official in the service of the archbishop of Trier, commenced on April 17. When he appeared before the emperor on the second day of the debate, Luther conducted a detailed defense of the books that he had written: "Some deal with faith and life so simply and evangelically that my very enemies are compelled to regard them as worthy of Christian reading. . . . A second class of my works inveighs against the desolation of the Christian world by the evil lives and teachings of the papists." Emperor Charles,

An heroic portrayal of Charles V wearing full armor and mounted on a warhorse. Such stylized renderings of Charles V fail to reflect the fact that his power was limited and that his nobles often failed to encourage full implementation of his policies.

who was by now uncomfortably aware of the fact that Luther was not about to pull his theological punches, grew restless. The next section of Luther's speech angered him even more. Luther spoke of the pope's tyranny over Germany and then made a statement designed to appeal specifically to German nationalism: "Should I recant at this point, I would open the door to more tyranny and impiety, and it will be all the worse should it appear that I had done so at the instance of the Holy Roman Empire."

In the final part of his speech, Luther admitted that his other writings had often been less than tactful: "A third class contains attacks on private individuals. I confess I have been more caustic than is suitable for a man of my profession, but I am being judged, not on my life, but for the teaching of Christ, and I cannot renounce these works either without increasing tyranny and impiety."

Von Eck, predictably, remained unimpressed: "Do not, I entreat you, Martin, do not claim for yourself that you are the one and only man who has knowledge of the Bible, who has true understanding. . . . Do not place your judgment ahead of so many distinguished men . . . as wiser than others." He then ordered Luther to put his case as clearly and simply as possible.

The situation was desperate. Neither disputant could conceive of the possibility that the other might be right. Both Luther and von Eck were appealing to more than 1,000 years of Catholic tradition. Luther felt that the Church had forsaken its original purity and, consequently, any supportable claim to authority, as far back in history as the 8th century. It was at this time, Luther believed, that the papacy had first begun to acquire an appetite for temporal power—an appetite, as it turned out, that could only be satisfied at the expense of spiritual concerns. Luther was basically a religious conservative, whose proposed reforms were intended to bring about a *renewal* of the Church. He wanted to see the Church as it had been when the precepts of St. Augustine had informed its very nature, or, even more ideally, as it had been during the first five centuries of its existence—solidly based upon the

A detail from *The Temptation of St. Anthony* by Dutch artist Hieronymus Bosch (1450–1516). Bosch's preoccupation with the monstrous and fantastic reflected the superstition that pervaded the religious awareness of many Catholics prior to the Reformation.

Gospels and the teachings of St. Paul.

While Luther was convinced that he had rediscovered the truth at the heart of the Christian tradition and that the leaders of the Church had defiled it, von Eck believed that the leaders of the Church were completely infallible and that no such desecration could have taken place.

Luther's final statements only served to emphasize that there could be no resolution of the dispute. On the following day, April 19, the Diet reconvened. As Luther sat alone in the lodgings that had been provided for him by the religious order known as the Knights of Rhodes, Charles's response was read out before the Diet: "It is certain that a single friar errs in his opinion which is against all of Christendom and according to which all of Christianity will be and will always have been in error both in the past thousand years and even more in the present. . . . I regret having delayed so long to proceed against this Luther and his false doctrine. . . . I am determined to proceed against him as a notorious heretic."

Despite the fact that the emperor had made his position clear, the princes and electors debated for another two days. They then requested that a small commission be appointed to continue examining Luther. The Diet's request was largely the result of the stand taken by Elector Frederick, who firmly believed that Luther had still not been proven wrong by the only authority upon which a proper verdict could be based—the Bible.

The princes of Germany now found themselves in an extremely difficult position. They could not afford to ignore the pope's condemnation of Luther indefinitely, and they did not relish the prospect of a direct confrontation with the emperor. Finally, they decided that Luther would have to go into hiding for his own protection. Working on the assumption that Luther would not have to face legal proceedings if he could not be found, the princes arranged to stage a bogus abduction, following which Luther would actually be taken to a place of safety. The princes felt that, once Luther was out of the way, the potentially explosive political situation

*If I had heard that as many devils would set on me in Worms as there are tiles on the roofs, I should nonetheless have ridden there.*

—MARTIN LUTHER
writing in 1545

that had resulted from the controversy over his teachings might yet be defused. Luther was to be taken to the Wartburg, a remote castle standing high up on a mountain overlooking Eisenach. The only other people at the castle would be the *castellan*, or keeper, and his family. Once he was at the Wartburg, Luther would have no contact with the outside world until his hair and beard had grown. Luther would be dressed as a knight and the few people who lived in the immediate vicinity would be informed that a noble landowner named *Junker* (knight) Georg had temporarily taken up residence in the castle.

Luther left Worms on April 26. Though he had grave misgivings about the ruse that had been devised for his benefit, he raised no objections. On May 4 Elector Frederick's soldiers captured him in a forest near Erfurt and brought him to the Wartburg.

**Luther is abducted by Elector Frederick's troops in a forest near Erfurt on May 4, 1521. Luther's abduction was organized by those German princes who were unwilling to hand Luther over to the authorities following his condemnation by Emperor Charles V.**

# 9

# The Exile

Even as Luther grew resigned to his solitary existence at the Wartburg, both the emperor and the pope stepped up their campaigns of condemnation. On May 26, 1521, Charles V issued a singularly violent proclamation to the electors, princes, and people of Germany. This proclamation, known as the Edict of Worms, called upon the Germans to forsake the dissident whose teachings threatened to divide the nation. Luther was now an outcast of both the Holy Roman Empire and the Roman Catholic church: "You shall refuse the aforesaid Martin Luther hospitality, lodging and bed . . . none shall feed and nourish him with food or drink . . . wherever you meet him, if you have sufficient force, you shall take him prisoner and deliver him (or cause him to be delivered) to us in close custody. . . . As for his friends, adherents, enthusiasts, patrons, supporters, partisans, sympathizers, rivals, imitators . . . we order that you shall attack, overthrow, seize and wrest their property from them, taking it all into your own possession. . . . As for the books of Martin Luther which our Holy Father the Pope has condemned . . . we order that nobody shall henceforth dare to buy, sell, keep, copy, print, or

In this simple chamber at the Wartburg, which he described as "the land of the birds," Luther wrote many letters to his friends in Wittenberg. Although he initially enjoyed the isolation, and even, on one occasion, described himself as "drunk with leisure," Luther eventually tired of his confinement and longed to return to the battle he had begun.

A satirical drawing of Luther as the mouthpiece of Satan. Such savage caricatures became increasingly common as the process of religious reform initiated by Luther eroded the power of the Catholic church throughout Europe.

**Luther and theologian Philip Melanchthon (right; 1497–1560) translate the Old Testament of the Bible from the original Hebrew into German. Luther, who wanted the translation to be comprehensible to all Germans, insisted that it should reflect the language used by "the mother in the home, the child in the street, the common man in the market place."**

cause them to be copied and printed, or approve his opinions, or support, preach, defend or assert them in any way. . . . We decree that . . . all in authority shall ensure that the works of Luther are burned and by this and other means utterly destroyed."

Emperor Charles V thus matched the pope's Bull of excommunication, which had undergone the revisions requested by Elector Frederick. In *Decet Romanum,* Leo proclaimed that Luther and his followers were "excommunicated, accursed, condemned."

The object of these verbal assaults spent much of his time alone in his room, which was situated in a side building of the castle. His small chamber contained but the barest essentials: a stove, a bed, a writing table, and a stool. The single, westward-facing window looked out over miles of forests.

Luther remained in communication with several of his closest friends from the very outset of his sojourn at the Wartburg. Messengers went back and forth between Wittenberg and the castle on a regular basis. Later that year his friends would even ensure that Luther's letters to the Saxon authorities reached the addressees. From his hideaway, to which he referred as "the land of the birds," he wrote to his friend Georg Spalatin: "I am sitting here all day, drunk with leisure. I am reading the Bible in Greek and Hebrew. I shall write a German tract . . . as soon as I have received the necessary things from Wittenberg." But Luther would eventually begin to despair of his isolation. He was extremely restless, anxious to join in the battle that he knew to be raging throughout Germany—a battle which he had begun and in which he imagined he could now have no part.

Though he enjoyed some aspects of life at the Wartburg, Luther was basically extremely lonely there, and occasionally suffered from periods of severe depression and sickness. In a letter to Philip Melanchthon, Luther wrote: "I did not want to come here, I wanted to be in the fight. The troubles of my soul have not ceased yet, and my previous weakness of faith still persists. I would rather burn in a raging fire than rot here alone half alive."

Luther did not allow his new circumstances to deter him from continuing with his scholastic pursuits. During this year Luther translated the entire New Testament of the Bible into German. The Germans already had numerous translations, but all of them were from the official Catholic Latin Bible, which had been translated from the original Greek and Hebrew hundreds of years before Luther's time. The translations from the Latin into German were

**The Wartburg proved a perfect place of refuge for Luther. While imperial troops scoured the countryside for him, Luther remained safe in his hideaway, dressed as a knight and known to the local people as Junker Georg.**

formal and somewhat awkward. Luther, fluent in Greek and Hebrew, set out to translate the Bible from the original languages. He worked with the Greek New Testament and eventually also translated the Old Testament from the Hebrew. Luther thought it important that the Germans have a Bible in their own vernacular, or everyday language. "You must not get your German from the Latin, as these asses do," Luther explained, "but you must get it from the mother in the home, the child in the street, the common man in the market place."

Luther began translating his German New Testament in December, 1521; it was first published nine months later. The complete translation of the entire Bible was to be published in 1534. Luther wanted the Bible "to be written in the simplest language so that all may understand it."

The captive also wrote numerous pamphlets at the Wartburg, particularly accusations against the pope, whom he called the "Prince of Hell." The insulting and abusive attacks by Luther were mirrored by angry Catholics, who would in turn publish similar treatises condemning the "crude and satanic" monk. When King Henry VIII of England read one of Luther's books he responded angrily: "What pest so pernicious as Luther has ever attacked the flock of Christ? What a wolf of hell he is! What a limb of Satan!"

While Luther was held prisoner at the Wartburg, the process of reformation that he had initiated began to accelerate. During his absence two extremists began to introduce new changes and slowly Luther's original reforms took on very violent aspects. Andreas Bodenstein (who was known as Karlstadt), a theologian at Wittenberg, and an Augustinian friar named Gabriel Zwilling, who also lived in Wittenberg, tried to persuade the populace that Luther had been too conservative and that more radical measures were necessary to change the Catholic church. Karlstadt and Zwilling began to advocate the use of force to overcome the old traditions. In July 1521 Luther received a written account of the discussion that had been conducted in Wittenberg concerning Karlstadt's theses on celi-

*Reason is the greatest enemy that faith has: it never comes to the aid of spiritual things, but—more frequently than not—struggles against the divine Word, treating with contempt all that emanates from God.*
—MARTIN LUTHER

bacy and communion. He was greatly disturbed by Karlstadt's proposition that all vows of celibacy were wrong. Luther believed that celibacy was an indispensable element of the monastic life. His own contention had been that celibacy could not reasonably be expected of those churchmen who were not members of the religious communities. To Melanchthon he wrote: "You people do not convince me that the vows of priests and monks are to be considered as in the same category." Luther had never entertained the prospect of seeking a wife, and Karlstadt's theses did nothing to change his mind: "Good Lord, will our people at Wittenberg give wives even to the monks? They will not push a wife on me!"

In November 1521 several friars left the Augustinian community at Wittenberg, never to return. Riots broke out. Priests were stoned as they led the Mass; convents were destroyed by students. Luther, fearing that the situation was becoming uncontrollable, decided that he would do well to go and witness for himself the latest results of his stand against the Church. In December 1521 he paid a flying visit to Wittenberg. From the conversations

ANNO · ETATIS ·    · SVÆ · XLIX ·

King Henry VIII of England (1491–1547), as portrayed by German artist Hans Holbein. Upon reading one of Luther's texts, the devout Henry became enraged, exclaiming "What a wolf of hell [Luther] is! What a limb of Satan!" During the 1530s, however, Henry was to break with Catholicism himself, establishing a national church in England.

Saint Benedict (480–547), the Italian churchman whose Benedictine Rule, governing monastic life and discipline, laid the foundations for the establishment of the religious order named for him. Unlike the Benedictines, who were confined to the monastery, Luther's order, the Augustinians, was committed to "passing on the fruits of contemplation" by working in society.

that he had with Melanchthon shortly after his arrival it became apparent that Spalatin, considering Luther's latest writings to be dangerously inflammatory, had failed to distribute them to the scholars at the university. Accordingly, Luther wrote to Spalatin expressing his surprise and disapproval.

Upon returning to the Wartburg, Luther wrote a pamphlet on the subject that had come to disturb him most during his journey to Wittenberg and back. He had become terrifyingly aware of the growing discontent and disquiet within Germany. His response to this threat of major civil disturbances was entitled *A Sincere Admonition by Martin Luther to All Christians to Guard against Insurrection and Rebellion*. This particular tract to some extent demonstrated Luther's essential conservatism and actually pleased many people in authority. Luther wrote that "no insurrection is ever right, however right the cause it seeks to promote . . . it generally harms the innocent more than the guilty. . . . I am and always will be on the side of those against whom insurrection is directed, no matter how unjust their cause. . . . Those who read and rightly understand my teaching will not start an insurrection; they have not learned that from me."

In February 1522 the Wittenberg town council took action. Without consulting Elector Frederick, the councillors wrote a desperate letter to Luther asking that he quickly return to help put a stop to the outbreaks of violence. As soon as he had finished reading the letter, on February 28, Luther began to pack his bags.

The entire Holy Roman Empire had heard the echoes of Luther's demands for the resurrection of faith as the central component of Christian belief. On his journey home Luther remembered the peacefulness that had characterized life in Wittenberg before the controversy caused by his teachings had come to capture the imagination of the people of Germany. It was fast becoming apparent that many of those who were eager for change had failed to realize that, when the desire for reform becomes an uncontrollable obsession, the consequences can be disastrous.

Luther as he appeared during his exile at the Wartburg, a remote castle near the town of Eisenach. During this period, he remained in communication with many of his colleagues and also translated the entire New Testament of the Bible into vernacular, or everyday, German.

A 16th-century engraving depicts **Pope Leo X** enjoying the luxury that he cultivated throughout his reign. The arrogance, corruption, and hedonism displayed by the high-ranking churchmen in Rome enraged the Germans, who resented the fact that the money they paid in taxes to the Church was ultimately used to finance clerical debauchery.

# 10

# The Swordsman

By returning to Wittenberg, Luther took a great risk. He realized that his enemies would now know where to find him. Outlawed by both the Church and the civil government, he could not avail himself of legal protection against the angry Catholics who rejected his teachings or the extremists who had chosen to use his doctrines of Christian liberty as justification for lawlessness. Following his return from the Wartburg, from March 9 through 16, Luther preached to the people of Wittenberg, trying to calm the radicals. He emphasized that Christianity was a spiritual quest, that what ultimately mattered most was the inner life. Luther criticized much of what had happened in Wittenberg during his absence from the town, declaring that "I would not have gone so far as you have done, if I had been here. The cause is good but there has been too much haste. . . . There are some who can run, others must walk, still others can hardly creep. . . . It looks to me as if all the misery which we have begun to heap upon the papists will fall upon us."

Despite Luther's appeal for moderation, it was apparent to Melanchthon that "the dam had broken," and that no one but Luther could "stem the waters."

**Such scenes as the one portrayed here—a noblewoman and her son begging for mercy—were common in Germany during the Peasant Wars of 1525. The peasants' revolt came in response to hundreds of years of political, social, and religious oppression that had left the lower orders of German society angry and resentful toward clergy and landowners alike.**

ALINARI/ART RESOURCE

**Philip Melanchthon, a close friend of Luther, was a brilliant theologian whose moderate approach to religious reform stood in great contrast to Luther's tendency toward vehemence and rigidity. In 1528 the Saxon authorities adopted Melanchthon's recommendations on church and school administration, thus creating the first public school system of the modern era.**

A member of the powerful de Medici family, Pope Clement VII (1478–1534) exercised a moderation that had been lacking in his predecessors. In 1525 he responded to the threat of the German religious reform movement by recommending reformation of the Church within the constraints of Catholic tradition.

In the sermon that he delivered on March 10 Luther declared: "I simply taught, preached and wrote God's word. And while I slept or drank Wittenberg beer with my friends . . . the Word so greatly weakened the papacy that no prince or emperor ever inflicted such losses upon it. I did nothing; the Word did everything. Had I desired to foment trouble, I could have brought great bloodshed upon Germany. But what would it have been? Mere fool's play."

Luther traveled to Erfurt, Weimar, and other neighboring towns to help pacify the brewing revolution, but his efforts often met vehement opposition. In the town of Orlamunde, for example, he was driven out "with stones and mud."

Among the radicals whose positions Luther considered both extreme and an affront to the spirit of his teachings, there were two who had particularly angered him—Karlstadt and Thomas Müntzer, a priest who had arrived in Wittenberg early in 1521, following his expulsion from the town of Zwickau, where he had delivered sermons that were little more than incitements to riot. Luther had already criticized Karlstadt's views on celibacy. He was also angry at Karlstadt's having encouraged the people to take the bread and wine in their own hands at communion, rather than from the hands of a priest. Throughout Germany, radicals like Karlstadt and Müntzer were using Luther's teachings as ammunition, often quoting him out of context in their efforts to provoke unrest.

In August 1522 Pope Adrian VI arrived in Rome from his native Netherlands. (Leo X had died in 1521.) Adrian's initial policy declaration was read out at the Diet of Nuremberg on January 3, 1523. A general demand for the suppression of heresy had been a feature of papal declarations for centuries, but Adrian felt obliged to make a specific reference to Luther, expressing both his surprise and his displeasure at the fact that the dissident from Wittenberg was still free and disturbing the peace of Christendom. The German nobles in attendance at the Diet were unimpressed by the pope's demands. They felt that the suppression of heresy could wait until Rome had put its own house in order and was no longer riding roughshod over Germany. Following the death of Adrian VI later that same year, another member of the de Medici dynasty became pope. Shortly after his succession, Clement VII sent an experienced papal diplomat named Lorenzo Campeggio to Nuremberg, where another Diet was in session. Cardinal Campeggio, displaying more astuteness than had several previous papal ambassadors to Germany, gave serious consideration to the reformist tendency that was developing throughout the country. As the Diet drew to a close, he persuaded the princes who were unsympathetic to the reformers to sign a declaration in support of reforming the Church *within* the constraints of Catholic tradition.

Campeggio's coup, while undoubtedly an out-

> *The mad mob does not ask how it could be better, only that it be different. And when it then becomes worse, it must change again. Thus they get bees for flies, and at last hornets for bees.*
> —MARTIN LUTHER
> writing in the aftermath of the Peasant Wars of 1525

standing example of diplomacy, demonstrated the extent to which Germany's religious divisions had begun to determine its internal political alignments. Around 12 months later it also became apparent that Campeggio's efforts to gain the allegiance of Germany's more conservative princes had not sufficed to stave off disaster.

The long-anticipated peasant revolt erupted in southern Germany early in the fall of 1524, and quickly moved north. The peasants used an image of a leather shoe, or *Bundschuh*, as their symbol. The word *Bund* meant both the lace of a shoe and a guild, or association. The *Bundschuh* acknowledged only two rulers, the emperor and the pope, and wished to abolish all intermediate rulers—lords of the manor, princes, electors, knights, bishops, and cardinals.

In February 1525 one of the leaders of the peasants wrote a treatise entitled *The Twelve Articles*, which listed the peasants' principal grievances. Among the demands set out in *The Twelve Articles* were the abolition of serfdom, the right to hunt and

A German peasant proudly bears a standard decorated with the symbol of the peasants' revolt—the *Bundschuh*. The word *Bund* meant both the lace of a shoe and a guild, or association. The peasants who marched beneath this banner during the Peasant Wars of 1525 acknowledged only two rulers—the pope and the Holy Roman emperor.

Peasants swear loyalty to the cause of revolution during the Peasant Wars of 1525. The banner (left) bearing an image of the crucified Christ attests to the religious zeal that many of the peasants brought to their bitter and bloody struggle against the rulers of Germany.

fish, and drastic tax cuts. The text was seasoned with appeals to the Bible and to Luther's doctrines. Luther's religious writings were thus given a social application. In another pamphlet the peasants asked Luther, Philip Melanchthon, and Elector Frederick, among others, to be their spokesmen. Despite the fact that he sympathized with many of the peasants' objectives, Luther refused to side with them when he saw the death and destruction that accompanied their revolt.

The peasants ravaged the countryside, killing local officials and sacking the castles of the nobility. Angry mobs destroyed 70 cloisters in Thuringia, and 270 castles and 52 cloisters in Franconia. Elector Frederick's brother (who would assume the electorate of Saxony following Frederick's death in May 1525) wrote, "As princes we are ruined."

When Luther tried to preach moderation to the peasants, he met with very strong opposition. The peasants believed that Luther was turning his back on them, that he was compromising under pressure from the government—which blamed Luther for the uprising. Finally, in May 1525, Luther wrote a famous treatise in which he publicly distanced himself from the rebels and made it clear that he did not consider the peasants to be true agents of reform. In this tract, which Luther entitled *Against the Murderous and Thieving Hordes of Peasants*, he wrote: "If a peasant is in open rebellion, then he is outside the law of God, for rebellion is not simply murder, but it is a great fire which attacks and lays waste a whole land. Thus, rebellion brings with it a land full of murders and bloodshed, makes widows and orphans, and turns everything upside down like a great disaster. Therefore, let everyone who can, smite, slay, and stab, secretly or openly, remembering that nothing can be more poisonous, hurtful, or devilish than a rebel. It is just as when one must kill a mad dog; if you do not strike him, he will strike you, and the whole land with you."

Luther's appeal was what the princes of Germany had been waiting to hear. More than 100,000 peasants died in the bloodbath that followed. Their leader, Müntzer, was eventually caught, and was subsequently tortured and beheaded. The princes spared almost no one—neither men, nor women, nor children; those to whom mercy was shown survived only because the nobles needed laborers to work on their estates. The Church wholeheartedly condoned the killing. When, for example, Bishop Conrad arrived in Würzburg, the town celebrated by executing 64 peasants. As the bishop traveled through the town with his executioner, another 272 people were put to death.

Now both the peasants and the Catholic church were angry at Luther. Because of his order to "smite, slay, and stab," the peasants saw Luther as a cruel traitor to the cause of the oppressed, while the Catholic church, not content with having labeled him a heretic, now declared him directly responsible for the bloodshed. In addition, German princes who had previously supported Luther were turning back to the Church. The Peasant Wars of 1525 had taken their toll.

In the wake of the momentous events that had taken place in Germany, many new religious fac-

*A mighty fortress is our God,*
*A bulwark never failing.*
*Our helper He amid the flood*
*Of mortal ills prevailing.*
—quoted from
"A Mighty Fortress is our God,"
one of the most famous of the
many hymns that Luther wrote

tions, with their own doctrines and leaders, emerged throughout Europe. As a result, Luther himself became less central to the ongoing reformation of the Church.

Many of the participants in the peasant revolt had belonged to a sect known as the Anabaptists. They believed that a person should not be baptized until he or she had reached "the age of reason"—Anabaptist terminology for intellectual maturity. The Anabaptists were individualists and considered the clergy completely unnecessary. They were violently opposed to luxury and ostentation and held that Christians should share their goods with each other. Of all the radical positions adopted by the Anabaptists, the most revolutionary was their denial of all distinctions of social class and their insistence that all men were equal before God.

The most important reformer in Switzerland was a scholar and priest named Huldrych Zwingli. Unlike Luther, Zwingli was not just a crusader for the renewal of the Church. From the moment of his conversion to the Lutheran cause, which took place

Luther preaches to the peasants. Horrified at the widespread carnage caused by the Peasant Wars, Luther attempted to preach patience and reason to the common people. However, the movement had grown so strong that even Luther was powerless to defuse the situation. When the imperial armies finally intervened, over 100,000 rebels were slain.

in 1519, he advocated a complete break with Catholicism. Under Zwingli's leadership, most of the population of northern Switzerland had deserted the Catholic faith by 1528. In 1531 the Zwinglian forces were defeated by the armies of the southern Swiss cantons (regions) and Zwingli himself was killed in battle. Under the terms of the Peace of Kappel, which was signed that same year, the Protestants agreed that the religion to be practiced in each region should be decided by the cantonal government.

Several years after Zwingli's death, another important Protestant movement originated in Switzerland. A scholar named John Calvin, suspected of heresy because of his interest in Luther's teachings, fled his native France in 1534 to avoid persecution. After spending some time in the city of Basel, he moved on to Geneva, where he began to preach. So charismatic was Calvin's exposition of his beliefs that by 1541 he had turned Geneva into a religious dictatorship that reflected his own theology. Calvin believed that, though all men were sinners by nature, God had predestined some (whom Calvin designated the elect, or chosen) for eternal salvation, and the majority for eternal damnation. Calvinism was much more radical than Lutheranism. Whereas Luther continued to acknowledge some features of Catholic worship and several elements of Catholic doctrine, Calvin was opposed to everything that he considered "popish."

Luther was to become increasingly disturbed by the splintering of the movement that had grown up around his teachings. Though he believed that everyone should be free to choose his own religious path, Luther did not believe that teachings other than his own could be acceptable to God. He advocated punishment for crimes against the state, for blasphemy, and for violent rebellion, but not for beliefs that he considered incorrect.

Luther's capacity for intolerance in matters of religion also found expression in his attitude toward the Jews, an attitude that has caused much controversy. Toward the end of his life, in 1541, Luther was to write a tract condemning the Jews that remains the subject of controversy to this day. Luther, like most Christians at that time, disliked the Jews because they were held responsible for the crucifixion of Christ. In this work, which he entitled *On the Jews and Their Lies*, Luther proposed that all Jews be returned to Palestine, their ancient homeland, and cited several passages from the Bible in support of his proposal. If that failed, he declared, then the Jewish people should be forced to support themselves solely from the land, their synagogues should be burned and destroyed, and the Church should confiscate all of their books, including the Bible. Luther's position on the subject of the Jews was largely determined by religion rather than race. Despite his spiritual motivations, Luther's attitude toward the Jews remains a prime, and sobering, example of his tendency toward intolerance.

A 15th-century painting depicts peasants at work in the fields while nobles stroll in a magnificent garden. Although the revolt staged by Germany's peasants in 1525 did little to change the social order, it served to convince Germany's rulers that their power was far from absolute.

# 11

# The Father

In the early spring of 1523, a student of Wittenberg observed that "a wagon load of vestal virgins has just come to town, all the more eager for marriage than for life." The twelve nuns in the wagon had escaped from a nearby convent with the help of Luther and an elderly citizen of Torgau, Leonard Kopp. Three had returned to their homes; nine were left to Luther's care.

By 1525 Luther had found either a home or a husband for all but one of the religious refugees. The remaining nun, Katherine von Bora, was almost ineligible for marriage by 16th-century standards: she was 26 years old. Luther tried to introduce her to many suitors, but none were acceptable. Defeated, Katherine jokingly insisted to a friend of Luther's, Dr. Nikolaus Amsdorf, the rector of Wittenberg University, that she would wed no one but Dr. Amsdorf or Dr. Luther himself—believing that neither option was possible.

Luther reported the amusing incident to his parents on a visit home. As an avowed "religious," he was committed to remaining celibate and had never contemplated marrying. As a condemned heretic, he realized that he might one day be put to death and that a man in such a position would hardly

ALINARI/ART RESOURCE

**Luther's wife, Katherine von Bora (1499–1552), as portrayed by Cranach. Von Bora, a former nun who forsook the monastic life following her adoption of Lutheran doctrines, married Luther in 1525.**

As the Reformation continued, Luther bemoaned the fact that, throughout Europe, many dissident churches had begun to call themselves "Lutheran." In one communication to his followers he protested thus: "I pray you leave my name alone and call yourselves not Lutherans but Christians."

make an ideal husband. However, when his father suggested that Luther take Katherine's jest seriously, Luther considered the possibility. Hans Luther wanted grandchildren—he had no desire to see the family name die with Martin. Luther himself reasoned that his taking a wife would spite both the pope and the Devil. And even if he were to be burned at the stake, his marriage would testify to his faith and the irreconcilability of his break with the Church.

On June 10, 1525, Georg Spalatin encouraged Luther to marry Katherine as soon as possible. Three days later Katherine and Martin were wed in a private ceremony—"an ex-nun and a renegade monk," as Luther put it. On June 27, 1525, the Luthers would have a gala public ceremony and

> *Sometimes we must drink more, sport, recreate ourselves, aye, and even sin a little to spite the devil, so that we leave him no place for troubling our consciences with trifles. We are conquered if we try too conscientiously not to sin at all.*
>
> —MARTIN LUTHER

party. Luther wrote to Spalatin: "You must come to my wedding. I have made the angels laugh and the devils weep."

On the morning of Luther and Katherine's public wedding, the bells of Wittenberg echoed through the small town. Katherine and Martin paraded through the narrow streets toward the old parish church, where they were married in public. After a joyous banquet at the cloister, the bride, groom, and guests gathered together in the town hall for a celebratory dance. The guests danced and dined until 11:00 P.M. That night, the newlyweds stayed at the cloister, where, much to their surprise, they discovered that the repercussions of Luther's teachings could even cause disturbances in the bridal suite. Luther's old opponent Karlstadt knocked at their door. He was

A bemused Luther accustoms himself to the distractions of life as a husband and father. Luther, who greatly enjoyed married life, once confessed, "before I was married the bed was not made for a whole year."

fleeing from the riots of the peasants and had nowhere else to turn.

Luther loved married life. As he observed, "before I was married the bed was not made for a whole year." To Luther, Katherine became "my lord, Katie," as he began to cherish her more deeply. Luther was often sick and Katie was an excellent home physician. The Luthers were to have six children: Hans (b. 1526), Elizabeth (b. 1527), Magdalena (b. 1529), Martin (b. 1531), Paul (b. 1533), and Margarethe (b. 1534). The children spent their days in a crowded household—eventually the Luthers housed 25 people under their roof. Students, the sick, four orphans, and monks and nuns who had left their orders found refuge with the boisterous and jovial family.

Students would gather around Luther at the dinner table, jotting down everything he said during the course of the meal. Their notes were published together in *Table Talk*, which has 6,596 entries. In it Luther talks about nature, the church, marriage, family, politics, and his own experiences. There was always laughter and good cheer at mealtimes—Luther had a great capacity for wine and beer—and the household always resounded with singing, amateur theatrics, games, and Bible reading.

Luther's enjoyment of his life as a husband and father was often marred by the intrusion of more serious considerations. Many hundreds of churches all over northern Europe were calling themselves "Lutheran" churches. Luther, however, did not approve of the fact that his name had thus become attached to the reformist movement that his teachings had inspired. He protested: "I pray you leave my name alone and call yourselves not Lutherans but Christians. Who is Luther? My teaching is not mine. I have not been crucified for anyone. . . . How does it befit me, a miserable bag of dust and ashes, to give my name to the children of Christ?"

By 1529, when the Second Diet of Speyer met to discuss the problems confronting the German state, the nation was already divided into Catholic and Lutheran provinces. If a particular prince was a

*For you may well believe me, one of his friends: Martin is much greater and more admirable than I could possibly suggest with words. You know how [the Athenian statesman] Alcibiades admired . . . [the philosopher] Socrates; I admire this man in an entirely different, namely, a Christian manner. Every time I think about him, he seems even greater to me.*
—PHILIP MELANCHTHON
contemporary and
follower of Luther

follower of Luther, then the churches within his domains were Lutheran. If he was Catholic, then the Catholic church was dominant within his territories. At the Diet, the Catholics supported Catholic liberty in the Lutheran provinces, but they did not advocate Lutheran freedom in the Catholic lands. Luther's followers reacted strongly, saying that they "must protest and testify publicly before God that they could consent to nothing contrary to his Word." The protesters thus came to be called Protestants—a label now used for all Western Christians who do not follow the teachings of the Catholic church.

Protestant churches were spreading past the borders of the Holy Roman Empire, westward into France, the Netherlands, England, Scotland, and Ireland, northward into Denmark, Norway, and

The ruins of Whitby Abbey, in Yorkshire, England, bear witness to the fact that the Protestant Reformation did not remain confined to Germany. In 1536, as part of his endeavors to establish a national church in England, Henry VIII issued a decree that dissolved more than 300 monasteries.

Sweden, and eastward into Poland, Hungary, and those parts of southern Europe that were then ruled by the Ottoman Turks. Following the Second Diet of Speyer, Emperor Charles V was preoccupied with waging war on the Turks and the French. As a result, he was not much concerned with domestic affairs. However, when he heard reports that increasing numbers of Protestant churches had been established within his territories, he decided to call a Diet and settle the growing problem.

The Diet of Augsburg met in April 1530. The Protestants were hoping that Charles would grant them freedom to worship in accordance with Luther's interpretation of the teachings of Jesus, and to do so in their own churches. Luther, since he had been condemned by the state, was forbidden to take part in the discussions. For six months, while the Catholics and Protestants debated, Luther lived at the castle in nearby Coburg, while Philip Melanchthon represented the Protestants.

From April to June Melanchthon prepared an official statement of Protestant belief, which was to become known as the Augsburg Confession. In consultation with other Protestant leaders, Melanchthon clearly set out all of the issues on which both groups agreed, and downplayed the more contentious aspects of the controversy. Though the first drafts of the Protestant statement (which Luther thought too compromising) contained many concessions, the Catholics were not willing to accept the document. They wanted the Protestants' deviation from Catholic belief to be as insubstantial as possible.

On June 25 several Protestant leaders signed a final draft of the Confession and presented it to Charles V. An official read the text aloud at a secret session the following day. After hearing the final doctrines, the groups debated for several weeks. Finally Charles V ordered the Catholics to draw up a similar statement. Dr. Eck, Luther's debating opponent at Leipzig, wrote the reply, which was read aloud on August 3, 1530. The heated negotiations continued. From his castle hideaway, Luther wrote hundreds of letters to his friends at Augsburg. "I

French theologian and religious reformer John Calvin (1509–1564). Persecuted for his interest in Luther's teachings, Calvin fled his native France in 1534, eventually settling in Geneva, Switzerland. His followers, who were known as Calvinists, were more radical than the Lutherans, seeking to eliminate everything they considered "popish."

would not yield an inch to those proud men, seeing how they play upon our weakness. . . . I am almost bursting with anger and indignation."

Despite the months of debate, the Diet voted on September 22 to reject the Protestant document in its entirety, thus leaving unresolved the deep split within Christianity. The Diet of Augsburg did, however, serve to unify the Protestant sects. In February 1531 Prince John of Saxony, who had succeeded Frederick as elector, proposed that the Protestant states form a defensive alliance. Negotiations were held in the city of Schmalkalden, in western Saxony, and the Schmalkalden League was established on February 27. The member states and cities of the League immediately began preparing to defend themselves against an attack by the Catholic princes.

In 1532 Charles V, several German princes, and 24 German cities concluded the Peace of Nuremberg. The terms of the treaty called for what was essentially a temporary relinquishment by the emperor of a number of his powers. It was agreed that any settlement of the religious issue would be effected, not by a Church council, but by a "free" and "Christian" council to be held in Germany. No date was set for the convening of such a council.

**Swiss religious reformer Huldrych Zwingli (1484–1531), who is regarded as the founder of Swiss Protestantism. One of the most radical figures of the entire Reformation, Zwingli espoused a complete break with the Church. By 1528, under Zwingli's leadership, most of the population of northern Switzerland had abandoned Catholicism.**

Due to the fact that Charles V then became preoccupied once again with fighting wars on the borders of his empire, no major confrontation was to develop until 1546, when the emperor returned. The war that Charles then waged against the Protestant princes lasted until 1555, when another Diet was convened at Augsburg. At this meeting, each prince was given the right to decide the faith of his province. The governing concept of the treaty was defined by the phrase *cuius regio, eius religio*—which meant that the religion of the ruler of a state would be the only religion permitted within the territory under his jurisdiction. Thus, the dissenters within each territory were forced to travel to a province where their faith was permitted. Lutheranism had finally achieved legal recognition in a number of German states. But Luther would not live to see this day.

After his marriage to Katherine, Luther continued to preach and to write letters, pamphlets, and hymns. He also continued to lecture at the University of Wittenberg and to assist his colleagues in the task of translating the Bible. People all over the Holy Roman Empire were reading his writings and singing his hymns in their churches. One of the most popular of these, "A Mighty Fortress Is Our God," is still sung in churches today.

In January 1546 Luther took his three sons to Eisleben, the town where he had been born, and then traveled on to Mansfeld to visit cousins and old friends, and to help settle some legal problems concerning the property and privileges of the town's ruling family.

On the journey Luther became ill. He suffered "palpitations of the heart" and shortness of breath. The work that Luther had to do for the rulers of Mansfeld was very demanding, and, in the end, it was to prove too much for him. On February 17, 1546, he suffered a heart attack. Early in the morning of February 18, in great pain but still in full possession of his mental faculties, he called for his sons and his companions. As he was very sick, they sent for warm towels and gave him glasses of brandy. He lay down on the couch and whispered,

"O Lord God, I am sorrowful. . . . I think I shall remain at Eisleben where I was born and baptized. O heavenly Father, if I leave this body and depart I am certain that I will be with thee for ever and can never, never tear myself out of thy hands." Luther then repeated three times: "God so loved the world that he gave his only begotten son, that whosoever believeth in him should not perish but have everlasting life."

As he closed his eyes, a companion asked him, "Will you stand steadfast by Christ and the doctrine you have preached?" "Yes," he said. "Who hath My Word," he slowly murmured, "shall never see death."

Luther was buried in the Wittenberg Castle church, close to the tomb of Elector Frederick.

The sense of loss felt by Luther's family, friends, and admirers, as well as their appreciation of his moral and spiritual authority, are perfectly conveyed in statements made shortly after his death by his wife, by one of Europe's greatest scholars, and by one of Luther's most trusted colleagues. In a letter she wrote to her sister in April 1546, Katie declared: "Who would not be sorrowful and mourn for so noble a man as was my dear Lord? Truly I am so distressed I cannot tell the deep sorrow of my heart to anybody and I hardly know what to think or how to feel. I cannot eat or drink nor can I sleep. If I had a principality and an empire it would never have cost me so much pain to lose them as I have now that our Lord God has taken from me this dear and precious man."

Erasmus, when informed that Luther was dead, expressed himself thus: "God gave the world in these later times when severe and acute disease and failures prevail, a harsh and severe doctor." And Philip Melanchthon, who had supported Luther and his cause for so many years, spoke for all those people who had found inspiration in Luther's teachings and in his personal example when he wrote that they were now "entirely poor, wretched, forsaken orphans, who had lost a dear and noble man as our father."

Even though more than 400 years have passed since Luther risked his life by refusing to compro-

> *Many loved him, many revered him, some were frightened of him, a few resentful. No one accused him, with any semblance of justification, of double dealing, or of cowardice.*
> —JOHN M. TODD

Luther on his deathbed, as portrayed by Cranach. The brilliant scholar and theologian whose teachings had inspired a generation of reformers died on February 18, 1546, at age 62, of heart failure, in Eisleben. His colleague Melanchthon later described himself and Luther's thousands of followers as "wretched, forsaken orphans, who had lost a dear and noble man as our father."

mise his beliefs, his teachings and the controversy surrounding them remain vital elements of the heritage of Western civilization. The political implications of the reforms that Luther inspired are still felt in Western Europe, especially in Germany. The policy programs of political parties in some modern democracies often reflect the religious affiliation of the majority of their members. Accurate predictions of regional voting patterns within a single country can often be made by taking into consideration which religious grouping—Protestant or Catholic—predominates in each region.

Martin Luther has even inspired one of the most celebrated plays to have been written in the English language this century. In 1961 British playwright John Osborne, author of the truly iconoclastic *Look Back In Anger*, further enhanced his own reputation as a powerful social critic with a play about the German friar whose criticism of the established order had brought about the Reformation. Osborne's *Luther* was hailed as a milestone in modern drama. It is, perhaps, not surprising that a revolutionary like Osborne should have chosen to deploy his abilities and sympathies to portray a revolutionary like Luther.

Lutheranism remains to this day a faith committed to opposing conditions that its adherents regard as unjust. The Lutheran churches in communist-ruled East Germany have been at the forefront of the anti-nuclear movement in that country for several years now. And it is not improbable that the father of Protestantism would regard such endeavors as fully in accordance with the spirit of his own. The story of Martin Luther remains a supreme example of the fact that one man's determination to follow the dictates of his conscience can tumble the seemingly immovable edifices of earthly power and change the course of history.

The Protestant princes of Germany defend their beliefs before Charles V at the Diet of Augsburg in 1530. Although the emperor had hoped that reconciliation would be achieved at the meeting, the two sides failed to reach an agreement.

# Further Reading

Bainton, Roland H. *Here I Stand: A Life of Martin Luther.* Nashville, Tennessee: Abingdon Press, 1977.

Haile, H. G. *Luther: An Experiment in Biography.* Garden City, New York: Doubleday & Co., Inc., 1980.

Luther, Martin. *Luther's Ninety-Five Theses,* tr. C. M. Jacobs. Philadelphia, Pennsylvania: Fortress Press, 1957.

Manns, Peter. *Martin Luther.* New York: Crossroad Publishing Company, 1983.

Pelikan, Jaroslav, ed. *Luther the Expositor.* St. Louis, Missouri: Concordia Publishing House, 1959.

Thulin, Oskar, ed. *A Life of Luther,* tr. Martin O. Dietrich. Philadelphia, Pennsylvania: Fortress Press, 1966.

Todd, John M. *Luther: A Life.* New York: Crossroad Publishing Company, 1982.

# Chronology

| | |
|---|---|
| Nov. 10, 1483 | Born Martin Luther, in Eisleben, Germany |
| Jan. 7, 1505 | Receives Master's degree from University of Erfurt |
| July 2, 1505 | Vows to become a monk following religious revelation |
| July 17, 1505 | Enters Order of Augustinian Eremites |
| 1508 | Summoned to Augustinian friary in Wittenberg<br>Commences teaching at University of Wittenberg |
| 1510 | Visits Rome |
| Oct. 18, 1512 | Receives doctorate in theology |
| 1513 | Leo X elected pope |
| 1515 | Luther appointed vicar provincial, becoming responsible for affairs of 11 Augustinian cloisters |
| Oct. 31, 1517 | According to legend, posts document containing 95 theses attacking central precepts of Catholicism to door of the Wittenberg Castle church |
| Oct. 1518 | Refuses to recant in meeting with papal representative |
| June 28, 1519 | Accession of Holy Roman Emperor Charles V |
| July 1519 | Luther questions papal infallibility during debate with theologian Johann Eck |
| June 16, 1520 | Leo X issues Bull *Exsurge Domine*, threatening Luther with excommunication |
| Dec. 10, 1520 | Luther burns *Exsurge Domine* |
| April 1521 | Defends his beliefs before Charles V at Diet of Worms |
| May 1521 | Exiled to the Wartburg, a remote castle, for his own safety<br>Pace and profundity of religious reforms initiated by Luther's teachings increase |
| March 6, 1522 | Luther returns to Wittenberg |
| Sept. 1522 | Publication of Luther's translation of New Testament into German |
| 1524–25 | German peasants clash with civil and religious authorities in conflict later known as Peasant Wars of 1525 |
| June 13, 1525 | Luther marries Katherine von Bora |
| April 1529 | Followers of Luther protest lack of freedom for Lutherans in Germany's Catholic provinces at Second Diet of Speyer, becoming known as "Protestants" |
| 1530 | Diet of Augsburg votes to reject Protestants' statement of belief, leading to permanent split between Germany's Catholics and Protestants |
| Feb. 18, 1546 | Luther dies, aged 62, of a heart attack, in Eisleben |

# Index

**Sally Stepanek,** a graduate of Yale University, is a free-lance writer and editor who lives in New York City.

**Arthur M. Schlesinger, jr.,** taught history at Harvard for many years and is currently Albert Schweitzer Professor of the Humanities at City University of New York. He is the author of numerous highly praised works in American history and has twice been awarded the Pulitzer Prize. He served in the White House as special assistant to presidents Kennedy and Johnson.

jBIO        Stepanek, Sally.
Luther
            Martin Luther.


$19.95   Grades 4-6

| DATE | | | |
|---|---|---|---|
| | | | |
| | | | |
| | | | |
| | | | |
| | | | |
| | | | |
| | | | |
| | | | |
| | | | |
| | | | |
| | | | |
| | | | |
| | | | |

BAKER & TAYLOR